Parents as Partners

Positive Relationships in the Early Years

by Jennie Lindon

Withdrawn

Updated to reflect the 2012 EYFS

D1437449

Published by Practical Pre-School Books, A Division of MA Education Ltd, St Jude's Church, Dulwich Road, Herne Hill, London, SE24 0PB.
Tel: 020 7738 5454 www.practicalpreschoolbooks.com

© MA Education Ltd 2009. Revised edition 2012. Illustrations by Cathy Hughes. Front cover image photo taken by Lucie Carlier © MA Education Ltd.

ISBN 978-1-909280-22-9

The meaning of partnership

The importance of partnership with parents has been confirmed in the revised EYFS (DfE, 2012). The statutory framework, with the welfare requirements, has been much reduced from the 2008 version. However, a significant aim is still that early years provision works closely with the families of young children. The first paragraph of the introduction states that, '*Good parenting and high quality early learning together provide the foundation children need to make the most of their abilities and talents as they grow up*' (DfE, 2012, page 2).

Best early years practice is grounded in partnership with parents, and other significant family carers. Early years practitioners should have expertise and professional insights to share. Part of your contribution to the partnership is that you will sometimes have knowledge about local services and specialist help, of which parents are unaware. An element of partnership continues to be the obligation to ensure that a young child's life does not end up fragmented. Practitioners need to make active connections between children's experiences at home and their time in early years provision.

Partnership over children

Effective practice recognises that partnership is a continual process, not something that can be established, like a one-off project, and then left alone. Partnership working relies on practitioners' relationships with a child's family, most often with the parent(s). The central aspects of the partnership therefore have to cover the following practice issues:

- Good, personal communication is crucial from the outset; from the time a parent makes an enquiry about your provision. Your relationship becomes established through the early conversations, as you explain what you offer and then, when the parent wants to take up a place, the further details.

- You work in partnership with a parent in order to ease the transition as a child settles into your provision. This process will include some joint time together with the baby or child in your home, as a childminder, or an agreed minimum time for a parent to stay with their child in a group setting.

- The settling-in process is for the emotional well-being of both parent and child. But it is also for a childminder, or the key person in a group setting, to begin to build a personal understanding of this baby or child. Although you aim to be

For many years now, good practice in services for young children has included a strong focus on bringing together the different parts of their life. In particular, practitioners within early years provision – the full range of group settings and the childminding service – have been expected to work closely with families.

Partnership within early years practice

The non-negotiable nature of partnership with parents is made clear in early years guidance across the UK. Establishing and maintaining close contact with young children's families is a professional obligation. This book is linked to the Early Years Foundation Stage (EYFS): the Birth to Five framework for England. However, the approach to good practice is consistent with principles which apply across the UK. For instance, the Care Commission in Scotland announced in 2009 that the focus in inspection will shift to reflect the details of the government's Early Years Framework. Part of this development is a greater emphasis on how settings actively involve parents and other family carers in their children's early learning, including any identified needs.

Think over what you do within your practice that you 'count' as partnership.

- The main focus for partnership needs to be on good communication and positive relations with individual parents. Do you give yourself credit for the effort you put into ordinary daily exchanges with a child's family?

- Childminders have much in common with the approach of a child's key person within a group setting. However, if you work from your own family home, you will not offer the range of events that might be organised by a nursery.

- Large settings, such as children's centres, aim to bring some services onto their site. However, this ambition is unrealistic for settings like a private day nursery or playgroup.

- Are you evaluating yourself against a sensible pattern for your particular service?

Food for thought

The essence of good practice is not so much the particular approach to the involvement side of partnership, but how practitioners develop an initiative and how they behave towards families. It is also crucial to keep a firm hold on positive experiences for babies and children. For instance:

- It would be irresponsible to develop a wide range of daytime events for parents, if that required taking practitioners away from the children.

- A welcome for parents within the day may have to be balanced against the impossibility for practitioners to share their attention between a young child and an emotionally needy parent.

- A wish to be flexible in meeting the needs of parents has to be balanced against the likely consequences for young children if that preference will create an unpredictable pattern of attendance from the child's perspective.

flexible, it would not be good practice to agree to next to no settling-in time, perhaps because parents say they have inflexible work commitments or they cannot see the point.

- A welcome for parents to stay occasionally with their (now settled) child or to arrive early to join the group for tea. This kind of open welcome is also a very clear message to all parents that their child is safe and happy with you. You have no reservations about the unscheduled arrival of a parent.

- Easy communication – between parents and practitioners as equals – about a baby or child's day and regular descriptive updates on an individual child's development. Regular conversation will be the way for anyone to raise any concerns – sooner rather than later – about a child's physical or emotional well-being, aspects of their development, or pattern of behaviour.

- Again, regular conversation will be the first option for practitioners to respond to queries or confusions from individual parents about what you do, how and why. Similar questions from several parents could let you know that there is a more general need for information and explanation.

- Good partnership includes a friendly end to the working relationship, as well as the beginning. A family's childminder or key person in a nursery should offer support for transition of the child and family from your provision and, as appropriate, onto the next provider or setting.

Partners – equal yet different

The main feature of working in partnership is that the different parties to the relationship feel equally valued, respected and able to be heard. Equal partners do not occupy exactly the same role in a child's life.

- Parents should be in a different relationship with their own children, in comparison with practitioners. Parents are more emotionally involved with their own children and looking ahead to a very long relationship.

- Parents and other family members need to be the continuity in children's life. Even young girls and boys, who have the good fortune to stay happily with the same nursery throughout their early childhood, will leave eventually. Children can have an even longer relationship with their childminder and some continue throughout their primary school years.

It is not a partnership if one side – parent or practitioner – believes they can simply direct the other person in the details of what to do or not do. However, neither does it feel like a partnership, if one side feels overawed or intimidated by the other. Young children can get lost as a consequence of either extreme.

- An imbalanced, one-way exchange can develop in provision where practitioners do the talking and parents are expected to listen and agree.

- Parents may appear to be content with this pattern – and silence is taken as agreement. However, they may feel intimidated or have no experience that makes them

question practitioners' behaviour. Alternatively, parents may judge that they cannot easily vote with their feet and find alternative provision.

- On the other hand, an imbalance can also develop when individual practitioners, or a whole team, have misunderstood the nature of partnership. I have listened to uneasy practitioners who believe that partnership requires agreement with just about whatever a parent asks.

- Some parents may be happy to take the approach that they are paying customers of a service and can ask for a highly personalised version of good quality care. On the other hand, a mother may simply be following an invitation to 'please tell me what you would prefer for Andreas'. Further conversation shows that she is very open to discussion.

Respect and partnership

Parents are people who happen to have children. Early years practitioners are fellow adults who work with children. It is unacceptable for either group to make sweeping statements about the other. However, practitioners have an additional responsibility as a professional; you should ensure that parents and other family carers are treated as individuals.

- It is not good practice to say, even in the limits of a team meeting: If only all the parents could be like Jamal's mother – she is so easy to talk with. A responsible discussion goes far beyond a wish list. What is it about Jamal's mother that practitioners find 'easy'? How can they take the responsibility for creating that feeling with some other parents?

- It would be very unprofessional to generalise from unhappy experiences with one or two parents to a criticism of 'the parents' as a whole. Practitioners need to think, or challenge each other to rethink statements like: 'The parents here are always complaining'. Produce some examples: whose parent, about what, and how was the situation resolved?

- Nor is it professional to talk about handling 'difficult' parents, as if the label is fully justified. What do you experience as

Links to your practice

You can be genuinely flexible when you, and your colleagues in a team, are clear about those areas of practice on which you cannot be flexible.

Sometimes, the best (and professional) option is to avoid giving a quick 'yes' or 'no'. You might say to a parent: "Thank you for explaining that you would prefer … Let me think about that. I will get back to you tomorrow".

It may not feel comfortable, but sometimes you need to say that you are not willing to meet the request that Tamara, just three years of age, is given writing practice every day. You give a professional reason: this activity is unrealistic for her age and will disrupt, rather than build literacy skills. You also offer any compromise that would be compatible with good practice – encouragement for meaningful mark making and more detailed feedback to Tamara's parent about her progress, which are directly relevant to sensible foundations for literacy.

'difficult' in your exchanges with this individual parent? What is the problem from your perspective as well as from theirs? How could you resolve this situation and what help might you appreciate from a colleague or advisor?

Who are 'parents'?

Good reflective practice leads you to check your assumptions. You may realise that you and your colleagues never wished to make anyone feel less than welcome. However, your practice is not as inclusive as you hoped and believed. No aspect of inclusion is ever resolved by claiming: 'But we treat all parents the same'. Full partnership recognises differences and you adjust your practice appropriately.

The word 'parent' means father just as much as mother, but sometimes fathers can feel less noticed or invited. There is no reason to suppose that you intended this consequence, but has your approach, timing or the way you describe events created the impression that you assume mothers will be your focus? You can recognise, and allow for, broad gender differences without sliding into an inappropriate 'one size fits all' for every father.

Over recent decades, men as fathers have become considerably more involved in the daily life of their babies and young children. However, many children are still mainly cared for by their mother. The early years workforce, and to a lesser extent the primary school workforce, is predominantly female. It is no use pretending that this visually obvious feature is unlikely to have any impact on the adults involved. Studies of partnership and fathers (Kahn, 2005 and Saunders et al. 2009) caution against any sweeping assumptions about fathers in general and reasons why (if) they are less 'involved' than mothers of young children.

Shared care systems within some families mean that several adults take a significant role within the life of a child who attends your nursery or comes to your home as a childminder. Practitioners need to understand how this family works and to respect the dynamics of a shared care family pattern – so long as it is working well for the children. However, your professional responsibility is to focus on the child and to ensure that communication is clear with parents. It is responsible to make clear that you need to know the family member who picks up a young child. Also you may take a different view about the minimum age that you judge it is safe for an older sibling to take a brother or sister in the daily transition from your responsibility to that of the family.

Some grandparents have an active role in the life of their grandchildren and sometimes this includes taking care of young children routinely. Early years practitioners may need to relate to a grandfather or grandmother (or other close relative) who regularly brings or picks up a child. Some grandparents take full responsibility for their grandchildren, because their adult son or daughter is unable to take care of the children – on a temporary or longer-term basis.

Links to your practice

Every member of staff in contact with families has to behave in line with the values of building positive relationships. For instance, it would undermine claims of working in partnership, if the manager of a day nursery ignored the fact that the cook was grumpy with any parents she encountered.

Millom Children's Centre recognised the important role of the receptionist of a busy, large centre. They reflected on the nature of the task and realised that at its core the role is about engaging and welcoming people 'in' to the centre.

The person at the desk in the reception gives families their first impression of your setting. S/he sets the tone of welcome, and is a source of reliable information as families become more familiar. Also that person is likely to hear a great deal – the chat as families come through, and their comments as they emerge from a workshop.

The person in reception has a vital role for talking and listening to parents, for picking up what people are really saying. So it is important to recognise how this role contributes to the development of trust, and ensure that there is appropriate support for the role.

The Pre-school Learning Alliance (www.pre-school.org.uk/fathers) encourages group settings to do 'The Dad Challenge', by keeping an accurate tally for a week of the family members who actually come to the setting. The PLA reports that there are often more fathers involved in drop-off and pick-up than teams predict.

I support this practical suggestion and add my own thoughts:

▪ How many fathers, and other male family carers, do you actually see within a typical week?

▪ Does the child's key person always greet fathers, as well as mothers?

▪ As the key person, can you think of something personal (not confidential) you know about this child's father – something that is a basis for friendly informal conversation? Is it easier to come up with a personal interest for the mother?

Some children are not in the care of their immediate birth family, nor living with members of their extended family. These children have become the responsibility of the local authority, with the status of 'looked-after children'. The children may return to their birth family, but it will depend on the circumstances. For the time being your partnership has to be with their foster carer(s) or their key person in a residential children's home (less likely with young children). Talk with this fellow practitioner and make sure you understand how the child refers to them – by personal name or that the child likes to use a family title such as 'Auntie'. Ensure that you understand the child's relationship with any other children in the home – are they siblings or not?

Hard to reach or overlooked?

Alma Harris and Janet Goodall (2007), in their review of practice in schools, raised the issue that some parents are categorised by professionals as 'hard to reach'. They pointed out that the perspective of some parents was that it was their children's school and the staff who were 'hard to reach'. Helen Wheeler and Joyce Connor (2009) acknowledged that some families live in circumstances that can make it harder to work closely with them. However, they describe how, in their Parents, Early Years and Learning (PEAL) training, they aim to find alternatives to the phrase 'hard to reach'. The phrase has come to be used very loosely to cover any family who appears to participate less, or is hard to persuade to get involved with what services currently chose to offer.

Example from a setting

Pound Park Children's Centre has applied an idea from the Pen Green Centre in Corby of undertaking socio-spatial mapping. This approach is to plot the postcodes of families who come to the centre for any services or special events. It is then possible to identify any gaps on an actual map of the local neighbourhood.

The team then reflect on how those gaps might have arisen and what could be done to gain a more even spread of involvement. The centre also has an Outreach Worker who makes contact with vulnerable families who are referred. Home visits are the vehicle for supporting these families, alerting them to suitable local services and encouraging their use of facilities based at the centre.

Age is sometimes felt to be an issue that complicates partnership. Parents may be close in years to their child's key person or childminder, but they could also be noticeably older or younger. Adults can become parents at very different ages – for the first or second time around. Your professional response needs to be consistent, whatever the parent's age, your own age and the extent of any gap. It is professional to avoid assumptions, which means you need to be honest with yourself.

▪ Is this parent being patronising, because she is quite a few years older than you? Or are you being over-sensitive, because you expect her to dismiss your expertise? Or is it a mismatch between her and your personality and age is irrelevant?

▪ Is this younger parent really being dismissive of you as 'old-fashioned'? Or are you interpreting her or his wish to 'think about' your suggestions as a swift rejection?

Being even-handed in partnership is not the same as treating all parents and family carers as if they are the same. It is good practice sometimes to aim directly at a particular group, when you have good reason to believe they could feel overlooked. Some early years provision has become aware that grandparents are closely involved in the life of their grandchildren and would welcome greater involvement in their early years provision. The same principles apply as for all partnership: talk with family carers who are grandparents and build a relationship with them through daily contact.

Once you get to know grandparents as individuals, you will have a basis for considering what they might welcome or like to offer within other forms of involvement. However, reflect on any unchecked expectations – from you or colleagues, if you work in a team.

▪ Do some quick sums in your head if you are thinking about childhood memories that grandparents may be able to share. Is what you have in mind more likely to be history than memory for this person?

▪ Avoid assuming that most people of grand parenting age will be skilled in 'traditional' crafts like knitting or growing vegetables. 'Older' women, of any cultural background, will not necessarily be good cooks and some 'older' men have never been able to put up a safe shelf.

- Alternatively, ensure any general 'we would welcome some help with … anyone who knows about … anyone who is able to …' are worded so that any family member is clearly included.

You will sometimes develop an event that is deliberately aimed at one group of parents or other family members – then choose a title that makes that focus clear. Wendy Scott (2009) reported on Ashbrow Infant and Nursery School in Huddersfield. Among the many aspects of active parent involvement was a fathers' group, known as 'Men Behaving Dadly', who amongst other projects had built an outdoor shelter in the children's garden.

Some local organisations and children's centres have developed drop-in sessions particularly for grandparents who are the main weekday carer of their grandchild(ren). Until you have successful word-of-mouth promotion, organisers need to think about how to promote the session. It is important to check your beliefs about what may be causing a low turnout.

- I have read reports of initiatives in which practitioners believed that grandparents could have no previous experience of drop-in groups. However, informal sessions like one-o'clock clubs were established in some areas by the mid-1970s, and even more by the early 1980s. Some parents from those decades are now grandparents.

- Another initiative was puzzled by the lack of response, but had illustrated their leaflet with an image of what the family support worker described as 'an elderly couple'. The report did not reproduce the image, but it does not sound inviting. Additionally, people who had their own children relatively young could easily be a grandparent by their early forties.

- However, it is possible that adults of grandparenting age may feel unenthusiastic in a group where everyone is significantly younger. Maturity in years does not necessarily bring increased self confidence.

Food for thought

Good early years practice is sensitive to the messages communicated by what is on your walls, including the visual images. It should be easy and immediate for any family to see themselves reflected in the resources you make available for children, and in any photos that are displayed.

However, in partnership, as in any other aspect of professional practice, a range of diverse images is not enough on its own. The Pre-school Learning Alliance and the Fatherhood Institute are both good sources for photos and posters that feature men as family carers. But, as both these organisations make clear, fathers will not feel more involved or consulted about their children just because a poster has been fixed to the wall.

In the same way, there is limited point in fixing up a multilingual 'Welcome' poster, if practitioners do not learn any of these words of greeting. Do you know which languages on the bought poster are actually spoken by families whose children currently attend your provision? There is no magical approach of partnership by poster.

Links to your practice

Some very young mothers, and fathers, are supported by their own parents in the parenting task. This relationship may work very well, but early years practitioners can get caught in the middle.

- Perhaps a young parent has become increasingly confident that she should make decisions about her toddler. However, her own mother has become accustomed to parenting a grandchild as well as her adolescent daughter.

- You may have to negotiate changes in the relationship over the time of your partnership. Alternatively, perhaps the young mother wants to use entry to nursery or the home of a childminder as a fresh start for taking the main responsibility for her child.

- Your aim as the key person is preferably to create the strongest family link with a child's parent. So even in a three-way settling-in period, make sure that you talk directly to the young parent and continue to invite her (or his) opinions and insight into the baby or toddler.

- You need to be diplomatic when other family members have been, or still are, significant carers. Perhaps you agree with Gemma's suggestion that her baby is ready for more than milk. That decision should not be overturned because the baby's grandparent disagrees.

In some cases, you will not have direct, regular contact with a child's parent or other family member. Perhaps there is another early years practitioner 'between' your setting and the family, for instance a childminder or the nanny employed by this family (or an au pair). You need to work in partnership with this other key carer in the child's life.

- So long as you have a clear agreement with everyone concerned, you can send some contact materials to the family via their childminder or nanny.

- A daily diary might travel this way, especially since your fellow practitioner needs to top and tail the record of the day. Standard letters or newsletters for all parents could be passed on by this route.

- However, more personal conversation about individual children, including any concerns, has to be communicated directly to their parent(s). You could use conventional post, email or talking on the telephone – all contact details that you should have from first meeting the parent.

- Clear requests of a need to talk could go by the same routes, as well as texting. It would not usually be appropriate to send this kind of message via someone else.

Example from a setting
Some provision offers transport for children to get between home and the setting. This facility is often very welcome when children have severe disabilities and especially if parents have to get other children to a different place.

Food for thought

'Parents' is a useful general term, but you need to behave as if it is always 'parents and other family carers'. It is unwieldy to keep saying, or writing, this phrase; but it is professional to keep thinking about different adults who take a parental role.

The main point is to avoid making assumptions. You cannot know everything about a family; that is why you need to have friendly conversations. A good rule of thumb remains: 'If in doubt, ask'.

It is not always easy to judge a family member's likely age. Once someone is well into their adult years, you are probably better to guess 'younger'. If it is not soon clear from conversation, then find out with: "I'm Marissa. I don't think we've met. Excuse me asking, are you Tom's Dad?".

An additional advantage of asking families for photos that you can laminate (as one of the tangible links with home) is that this store in a child's personal basket may solve your problem. You will be able to say: "I'm Neela and I recognise you from your picture. You're Morag's Auntie Peg. She loves looking at the photo of you and her feeding the ducks".

Links to your practice

If you want a flexible session to feel inclusive of different family members, then it is wise to think about what you call the event.

- 'Parent and toddler drop-in' is going to sound as if the organisers only have actual parents in mind.

- 'Sums for Mums' is a snappy title for an early maths workshop, but it risks sounding as if mothers are the main, or only, target.

- Think about other possible descriptions, perhaps 'Stay and play', 'Yes, everyone can do maths!' or 'Paint and chat'.

- Then it is important that every person who walks through the door is actively welcomed. Practitioners need to take the lead on this warmth.

In Petts Wood Playgroup for children with special needs the mini bus driver and escort are an important part of contact with some families. The role of these volunteers is to ensure good communication with parents with details about their child's time today at the playgroup session. A contact book also travels to and fro and gives a written description of what a child has done and any issues about their health and well-being. These are not the only channels of communication, since parents are welcome to telephone the playgroup leader and to come to the termly open mornings.

The importance of home learning

Various official reports and guidance emphasise the importance of family and home life in early childhood, as well as good quality experiences in out-of-home provision. This approach for good practice is confirmed as a professional obligation within the EYFS:

Close working between early years practitioners and parents is vital for the identification of children's learning needs and to ensure a quick response to any area of particular difficulty. Parents and families are central to a child's well-being and practitioners should support this important relationship by sharing information and, as appropriate, supporting children's learning at home (DfE, 2012, paragraph 1.11).

One long-term study, the Effective Provision of Pre-school Education (EPPE) identified a strong influence of the home learning environment (HLE) on young children's intellectual and social development and has tracked the continued impact through those children's primary school years. The team developed a measure of HLE from what parents said they did with their young children. These shared activities included reading to and with the children, singing, going to the library and other local visits, painting and drawing and playing with letters and numbers.

The home learning environment was, and continued to be, more significant for the child's development and school achievement than using predictions from the family's social class or the parents' own educational level. In different reports the EPPE team describe the situation as 'what parents do with their children is more important than who parents are'.

The overwhelming practical lesson of the EPPE research is that any approach to

Reviews of research (like Harris and Goodall, 2007 or Desforges and Abouchaar, 2003) into the impact of home on children's learning are honest that it is hard to unravel exact cause-and-effect. One complication is that people use a general term like 'involving parents' to cover very different initiatives.

However, the beneficial impact of home learning seems to work because children develop a positive concept of themselves and view themselves as a learner. Their parents have high aspirations for them and feel able to contribute to the learning within the family.

Parents feel like they are working with, rather than separate from or against, their child's early years provision or school. Neither early years nor school provision can do everything; secure learning needs family input, and the consistent message from parents is that the effort is worthwhile.

encouraging parents' engagement in their children's learning has to lead from a genuine respect for how family life runs.

- Initiatives to support home learning will not be well received if the underlying message is that parents do nothing much with their children until persuaded by early years professionals.

- A starting point needs to be that professionals show themselves willing to hear about and understand what parents do at home – often more than early years or school practitioners realise (Brooker, 2002).

- With knowledge of family learning – often gained by informal conversation – practitioners are then in an appropriate position to make connections between what they do in their early years provision and what parents could do, or are already doing, at home and in their own way.

- Sometimes parents are doing much more than they believe, because they do not classify domestic and other shared activities as 'proper learning'. Early years practitioners need to explain how important skills, such as early literacy and numeracy, flourish in the meaningful context of making real shopping lists or laying the table for a family meal.

- On the basis of their knowledge of child development, practitioners can be valuable in sharing realistic expectations, for instance about early social skills and the limited ability of very young children to 'share', in ways that adults mean that word.

- A childminder or key person may be in a good position to chat about a topic that has been covered in the national media, such as boys and literacy. This opportunity may be perfect for a few suggestions about the kind of books that Ansel enjoys in the setting, and that he is definitely interested in information books and action stories.

Links to your practice

In 2002 Liz Brooker reported a detailed case study of one reception class in a primary school in the east end of London. Among the many interesting details, she describes three practice issues that deserve reflection for any team.

- The reception practitioners were very sure that they were always available for easy conversation with any parent. However, this open-ended approach did not lead to equality of communication across the families. Some parents were comfortable to approach staff, whereas some parents would have welcomed a situation in which staff directly engaged them.

- There was a great variety in what the families sought to teach their children at home. The staff had limited knowledge of what parents did with their children at home.

- Parents also varied in their understanding of the play-based approach in the reception class, and their own childhood experience could have been very different. This puzzlement about how children allegedly learned through play was especially marked for families who were Bangladeshi in origin.

Relationships and communication

Partnership rests upon your commitment to establish and maintain a friendly working relationship of partnership with parents. Many parents are equally committed to making a strong, positive relationship with their childminder or key person in an early years group setting. Most parents want to feel a friendly connection with the person to whom they entrust their baby, toddler or young child. The positive tone is set by practitioners, who recognise that parents are entering the 'territory' of someone else, whether the family home of a childminder or a group setting. It is a professional responsibility for practitioners to offer an active welcome.

Friendly yet not friends

Early years practitioners, just like school and out-of-school practitioners, need to aim for a friendly relationship with parents and other family carers. Nevertheless, it is still a working relationship; practitioners and parents have not come together because they have chosen each other as friends.

There may be issues to resolve over differences between a friendly professional and a friend. It is not appropriate to behave in the same way in the two roles.

- It is inevitable that you will feel more comfortable with some individual parents, and they with you. But you have a responsibility to judge priorities in your work in a professional way and not to spend more time with some parents, nor to avoid others, because of your feelings of comfort or unease.

- Partnership with parents ideally includes some relaxed conversation; it is not exclusively about the details of childcare and development. Sometimes you will return to something a parent has said in passing. You ask how a mother's country walk was last weekend or whether a father feels better after his bout of flu.

However, this professional patter is different from a friendship. You need to maintain a responsible balance over confidentiality and passing on information.

- Perhaps several parents could not help but hear how Gary's mother was verbally abusive to you yesterday afternoon. It is understandable that they may comment, if only to ask: "Are you OK?".

- As friends, you might discuss the incident at length. In your professional capacity, you need to limit it to: "Thanks for asking. Yes, the conversation did get heated". If you sense more questions may follow, you might add: "But it's resolved now".

Professionalism requires a combination of commitment and detachment (or distance). At first glance this statement may seem to be a contradiction, but please reflect on what your job asks of you.

- You need to be emotionally and intellectually committed to young children and their families, to do your best for them day by day. You should not vary what you offer depending on your mood, nor on your first impressions of a child's family carer. Perhaps you have quickly warmed to Susie's father, who seems to trust you. Then you struggle not to

Links to your practice

Supporting guidance that accompanied the first version of the EYFS (in 2007) stressed the importance of partnership as an ongoing relationship between practitioners and parents. However, discussion also raised the sensitive point that professional relationships are based on friendliness towards parents, which is different from friendships. This key point could be as a focus for discussion within a team or childminders' network meeting.

- The issues are not new; since my training and consultancy from the 1980s I have raised the difference between a friendly working relationship and a friendship.

- Practitioners need, and deserve, support to negotiate the sometimes uncertain boundaries, especially within a profession that places a high value on nurture.

- It is not good practice (as I have occasionally heard from unreflective practitioners) that their years of experience enable them to 'know' those parents who will not take advantage, if the rules are bent for them.

In your team have there been differences of opinion about given situations? Is there a risk that some parents experience a different service, only because they are judged to be trustworthy or nice? If you work alone, do you have someone with whom you can discuss these professional issues?

Links to your practice

Everyone has a right to a life outside their work and, for the most part, it is not for a team leader or other professional to comment upon a practitioner's private life. However, everyone has the responsibility to ensure that they do not behave in their personal time in ways that undermine their professional role, nor risk bringing a whole team into disrepute.

The wide use of social networking sites has raised a new aspect to the boundaries between work and personal life. The Internet is essentially a public forum and not a private conversation.

■ It would certainly be unacceptable professionally for practitioners to post remarks about individual children, parents or colleagues from their work.

■ There is anecdotal evidence that some team leaders have had to address the consequences when practitioners have welcomed a parent as a named 'friend'.

■ Practitioners should not use their own camera or camera phone for taking images within their work. So there should be no possibility of posting photos of children onto a social networking site.

■ Have you discussed these issues in your provision? If not, should you?

dislike Euan's grandmother, whose endless questions seem to challenge your expertise.

■ However, you need to be able to step back sometimes: to realise what needs to be said, even if it may not be welcome to a parent. You will find a courteous way to express your concerns about Damian's language development. But it would not be professional to hold back for fear of 'upsetting' or 'annoying' Damian's mother, who is certain her son 'understands everything'.

■ You may wish to avoid a punitive approach to time keeping. However, the majority of early years provision does not offer an open-ended service. You appreciate the work pressures on Erin's mother, but not to the point of letting her believe it is acceptable to arrive late most evenings.

Example from a setting

The members of the Charlton Childminding Network were thoughtful about the nature of partnership in the childminding service.

■ **Some parents specifically wanted a childcare option that meant their children spent time in another family home. There was an advantage that the relationship could work like an extended family.**

■ **The most usual situation is that childminders are sole practitioners. Some parents choose a particular childminder as much for their own belief of, 'I could get on well with this person' as for confidence in what would be offered to their child(ren).**

■ **Childminders themselves explain that, in the long relationships that can develop, they may become more like friends with a family. As Georgina Mellish-Laws explained, she has had some children 'from the scan' – in that a family has committed to a place with her at an early stage in the pregnancy. Several childminders described that what could be years of close contact does not always end when an older child no longer needs the childcare service.**

It is worth pointing out that the role of the key person in a group setting is absolutely supposed to be that of creating a close relationship with each family. The clear message of the EYFS is that all early years provision should strive to be home-like.

> Be clear about your core values

There will always be some potential imbalance between practitioners and parents, or other family carers. Childminders and practitioners in group settings are responsible for following the policies that underpin good professional practice. No practitioner can flex on key values, however strongly a parent might feel to the contrary. Good practice in partnership has to be that, as a sole practitioner or a member of a nursery team member, you know what is negotiable with parents and what is not.

For instance, part of your early conversation(s) with a parent is to understand in what way family beliefs have a direct implication for your taking good care of their son or daughter. These beliefs may be linked with the parents' cultural background and this applies to everyone. Alternatively, the family's viewpoint may be shaped by a specific religious faith. Conversation is your chance to ask suitable questions, rather than risk assumptions.

Perhaps the family's preference over food is straightforward for you to implement and you have a practical conversation about clothing that is suitable for active and potentially messy play. However, partnership does not mean agreeing to whatever parents ask – whether from the first conversations or a strong preference that emerges later in the working relationship. It does not matter how strongly parents express their views, nor that what they say is the basis of their non-negotiable request, sometimes you will have to say: "I will not be able to agree to … because…".

For instance:

- You cannot agree to a condition that their child does not play outside unless the parent is satisfied each day that the weather is acceptable. Good practice is that children spend generous amounts of time outdoors, equipped with suitable clothing for the time of year and shelter against sun or rain.

- You could never agree to any parent's request that their child should not play with other children who differ in ethnic group or faith from the family. Nor should you ever imply – perhaps by not acknowledging the issue openly – that a child will not have contact with given team members.

- You should have a clear policy over positive approaches to guiding young children's behaviour. Good practice in partnership means that you discuss issues with a parent, so you can be as consistent as possible between this child's familiar people and places. However, you cannot follow family requests that would mean handling a child's behaviour in a way that was emotionally or physically harsh.

A vital element in partnership will always be to explain to parents at the first meeting (through conversation and written material about your service) how some aspects of practice are non-negotiable. Further conversation will be necessary later, if events lead to potential disagreement. When parents and practitioners hold incompatible views with equal conviction, a discussion will not be easy but can be possible. Honesty, tact and respect for views which you do not share may help to bring about a working acceptance. In the few cases when compromise proves to be impossible, then parents have the right and choice to remove their children. Nursery childcare does not suit the needs of all families; parents have the option to use the childminding service or employ their own nanny.

Food for thought

The distinction between being friendly and being a friend can become a sharp issue when you live in the same neighbourhood as where you work. The possible blurring of boundaries can become even more acute if you grew up here and some of the parents of your service are actual friends in your personal life. Your professional role means that you have to step back a little and to be very clear in your own mind over the limits to open communication with friends on some topics.

- It may feel irritating within a social situation. But you have to opt out of usual conversation between friends, when it veers into talking about children who attend your nursery or club – or their parents' life.

- Some practitioners find it useful to make the firm but friendly distinction of: "Now you're looking at Jan the childminder. You know I won't talk about local families in this way".

- Notice that the word is 'won't': Jan has chosen to make this decision. The word 'can't' gives the unprofessional message that somebody else is stopping her, and maybe she could be persuaded into gossip.

- Have you, or colleagues, faced this kind of situation? What did you judge were the main issues? How did you resolve the dilemma?

Links to your practice

Government policy has taken the stance that early years provision should be as flexible as parents require – in part so that they can take up paid work. However, there is a limit to how far the childminding service or early years group settings can meet the variable, random or non-regular hours that suit some families.

There can be issues about total hours of work for staff and an effective key person system in group settings. However, endless flexibility of attendance also raises serious questions about the well-being of young children, who need a fair level of predictability in their non-family time. Some private day nurseries I know have thought seriously about establishing a minimum amount of time that a child will attend each week, as well as how much variability in terms of which days. Informal drop-ins are a different situation, since children remain the responsibility of their accompanying parent – or childminder.

How do you approach this aspect of good practice for children and partnership with families? You need to be clear about your boundaries, so that you can explain the limits to what you offer and your reasons.

You may be a childminder, whose key values do not suit a family. Again there will be other childcare options locally.

Example from a setting

All early years practitioners need to assess whether there is too great a gap between what a family wants and the boundaries to the service offered. It is responsible to acknowledge as early as possible any differences that could easily become a conflict between incompatible ways of raising children.

■ **The Charlton childminders talked about their strong motivation to find a compromise whenever possible, especially if a family was in pressing need. However, there had to be some manoeuvring room, both for consistency with the core values of the service and attention to the needs of other children.**

Several issues have arisen in my conversations with practitioners in nurseries, as well as childminders in their own home.

■ **Some areas of potential disagreement, like wariness about outdoor play have been overcome through careful explanation and negotiation**

over suitable clothing. The discussion has been friendly, but nevertheless the message continues to be that the children will spend a considerable amount of their time outdoors.

■ **Some differences of approach have not been feasible to resolve, unless a parent will compromise. Good practice for a key person/childminder is to provide continuity with a baby's routines at home. However, it is not possible to follow a very strict routine (the example given to me has been Gina Ford's schedules) without serious impact on the routines and choices of other babies.**

Practitioners need to be ready to explain, in a positive way, aspects of their practice that may surprise or puzzle some parents.

■ **Carole Allen and Ellen Edwards – two Charlton childminders, who were closely involved with the Forest School project – described how their general practice had moved much more to being led by the children's interests. Their own homes had plenty of open-ended resources, but they needed to be able to talk with parents about why they did not have lots of bought toys.**

First contacts

Partnership will not work if it is little more than a paper promise. A genuine partnership between parents and practitioners has to work as part of a continuing, friendly relationship between the centre and parents. First contacts are important, since first impressions can be powerful.

Example from a setting

The Charlton Childminding Network meets weekly at the Pound Park Children's Centre. Childminders attend with their minded children and the session combines play for the children with social contact for the minders. The session is also open to parents, who have found the opportunity a good chance to meet local childminders informally. Kim Bush, the network co-ordinator, described how some parents had been able to move towards choosing a childminder for their child, and then following up with contact with that individual at their own home. However, the relaxed morning had also given some parents a better understanding of childminding and a basis for deciding how to choose between this option or a nursery place.

Petts Wood Playgroup (PWPG) for children with special needs has been running a service since 1968 for local families whose young children have a range of special needs. A full-time leader and deputy are supported by a predictable rota of volunteers.

■ A key aim of PWPG is to work closely with parents from the earliest stage of a referral, which can be that parents self-refer their son or daughter. Some aspects of partnership are common strands of good practice for any early years setting. Other aspects are particular to effective support of families with one, or more, children with special needs.

■ Parents are welcome to visit before deciding that the playgroup will suit their child. They are also welcome to stay with their child in a session if they wish. This option has been reassuring for a parent, when their child – even if long settled into the playgroup – goes through a period of feeling unsettled.

■ When I spoke with parents during an open session, they talked about an overall sense of welcome and the flexibility over days of attendance. Partnership is an integral part of considering how a child's pattern of attendance could change over time or dovetailed with time spent in a local mainstream nursery, when that is an appropriate option.

There is now a long tradition in some group settings of offering a home visit to families as part of the earliest contacts. This visit is offered when the family has accepted a place for their child and the key person has been allocated. A home visit can be a very positive beginning to the working relationship. However, parents can, of course, say 'no', that they would rather meet in the nursery.

■ Many parents are comfortable to be literally on their home ground. Conversations can be informal and cover some of the information that parents need to understand, when they are new to a provision. But it is never wise to attempt to cover everything in one go.

■ The home visit, or first visit to a childminder or nursery, is the time when a child's personal information record is started. Many practitioners use an informal 'All about me' record, which is completed from the child's perspective, such as 'I live with…', 'What I like to eat' or 'How I like you to help me in the toilet'.

■ A more structured form can be the vehicle for information like contact details, full names of family members, special needs, language(s) spoken in the family home, cultural background and implications for details of care and so on.

■ You need also to ensure that you get the personal and family names right for everyone: how you spell each name and how you say it, if the pronunciation is not obvious to you.

■ Good partnership is shown when you are ready to explain simply to parents why you are asking questions and can make the link with taking good care of their child. You want to understand other parts of the child's life – for instance, that Jamal spends most weekends with his Dad, or that Morag's Auntie Peg will take care of her on the two days she does not come to nursery.

■ An advantage of the home visit is that the key person sees children in their home surroundings. Later partnership may

A positive first contact and good continuing relations make it more likely that parents will trust you with details about their home life. It will help your care of Gita to understand that her beloved grandfather is seriously ill, or that Dan's uncle has just gone to prison.

Practitioners who work on or close to military bases are aware of the impact on family life when one, or both parents, are employed in the armed services.

■ Partnership includes support for parents who are anxious about a spouse on active service in a war zone, as well as understanding the behaviour of children who miss a parent.

■ The situation may arise that children are in the care of a grandparent, because both parents are now away on active duty in a war zone.

■ The network of service families can be strong. Early years practitioners may themselves have a partner in the services, and understand the extent to which families can move around the country on a regular basis.

■ It is normal life for the children but raises issues, of which practitioners need to be aware. In the same way as for children in families where one parent travels a great deal and is away from home.

be more effective because the key person has a greater understanding of the family circumstances.

■ Children also treasure the memory that their key person, 'came to see us' or 'saw my cat and my garden'. Their later recall in conversation can remind you of the importance they assign to this connection.

Practitioners have to be cautious not to draw swift conclusions from the home visit. Some parents may feel confident about talking with you and asking their own questions. But others may be wary, despite having agreed to the visit. You are an early years expert and – however friendly you are – some parents worry that you will judge them. Experienced practitioners realise that a lack of toys may mean this parent is concerned for you to see a tidy home. Children may be told to keep quiet, because the parent wishes you to think a son or daughter is well-behaved. The home visit, as much as the settling-in period when a child starts with you, is the beginning of a relationship in which you communicate what you value for young children.

Whatever the location of the first meeting, part of establishing firm foundations to partnership has to be a written agreement about the service. This commitment on both sides is a clear statement of what you offer such as the pattern of attendance, whether you provide lunch and other practical details and what is expected in return such as payment of fees and time keeping. Childminders need this kind of clarity as much as group settings.

You can find examples of agreements from professional organisations for the different types of early years provision and sometimes local advisors have samples of what they suggest. This agreement is also the time to obtain general permissions from parents for your usual range of local outings and for taking photos within the setting. You should ask for separate permission for special outings or any other use of photos.

Sharing the care of young children

A key person approach for nurseries has long been regarded as best practice. In 2007, the EYFS for England made it a legal requirement that each child must be assigned a key person. The revised EYFS in 2012 has confirmed this non-negotiable standard, and that for the childminding service, a childminder is the key person to a child and family. The revised statutory framework (DfE, 2012, 1.11 and 3.26) remains very clear: the key person should develop a continuing, personal relationship with individual babies or children and their family.

■ Close partnership with families is a central strand of good practice across early childhood provision. However, good communication between the key person, or the childminder, and parents is especially crucial with babies and toddlers.

■ Does this mother plan to continue to breastfeed? Would she like to provide expressed milk, or actually come into the provision to breast-feed? Does the family have a clear stance about kinds of food, when the time comes for weaning?

- Day-by-day good practice is that the key person shares a child's day with his parent, and that this open communication is definitely as detailed for fathers who pick-up their baby or child as for mothers.

- Either parent, or both together, are welcomed to connect what happens in your provision with what happens in family life. By spoken communication and the events of a daily diary (or whatever you like to call this record), parents get a clear image of what engaged their child's interest today, as well as physical details like eating and sleeping.

- Full and easy communication, beyond the settling-in period, reassures a child's parent, or grandparent, that you respect and want to draw on their expertise about this individual young boy or girl.

Example from a setting
The early days and weeks of contact will be the way to continue to show parents and children that you directly value home life and want to create visual as well as conversational links.

- **In Grove House Children's Centre, the personal portfolio for each child often starts with photos from the home visit. If parents are happy for those photos to be taken, everyone including the child has a visual record from the very beginning of this personal story.**

- **In Grove House Infant and Toddler Centre, young children have easy access to personal books that have been made for each child. These books include photos of family members and pets, with a caption explaining names and family relationships. Toddlers love browsing their own book, but it was noticeable that these very young children were also interested in looking at each other's book.**

- **In Buckingham's Nursery School, each family is invited to provide family photos that they can spare. The photos are laminated and ribbons fixed to either side of the upper edge. A collection of these photos is available for each baby and hangs on their personal peg for mobile toddlers. In much the same way as in Grove House. The older babies, toddler and twos are keen to look at their own family photos and those of their friends.**

- **It is usual good practice for any early years provision that individual children have their own drawer or personal basket. This store provides a safe place for personal possessions, which often includes important items from home, which young children handle when they want a direct connection.**

- **In Sun Hill's reception class a whole wall is filled by an impressive array of shoe boxes. The children call them 'cubbies' (from 'cubby hole') and these boxes are used for safe keeping of notes to go home and for children's personal items. Families whose child is due to start at Sun Hill are given a shoe box, with part of the lid ready cut away. Children are invited to personalise it however they wish. On their first day, children bring their unique container. The team are**

Links to your practice

The aim of a settling-in period is to reassure the parent as much as ease the experience of a baby or child. It is helpful if the key person is willing to accept being shown by a parent what she or he would prefer.

You may be an experienced childminder who has lost count of how many bottles you have made up and babies who have happily fed in your arms. But Tasha's mother will feel so much better, if you are gracious about watching her demonstrate to you how she does it at home.

Maybe Sachin's father does know more than you about using cloth nappies, since your nursery has only recently switched from disposables. This father knows not only how to fold a nappy for his especially small baby, but also why you fold one in a different way for a boy than a girl.

Links to your practice

It is good practice to have written material about your service and it will not necessarily be very long, especially for a childminder.

- Think about the key points you need to make and choose your words so that they can be understood by fellow adults who are unlikely to share your specific early years expertise.

- Lay out the content so that different sections are clear and make sure that everything is spelled correctly.

- If you have a website, then take the same amount of care over the information and ensure that it is updated as necessary. If someone else creates the site for you, then you need to be closely involved in the details.

- If you have images, such as cartoons or sketches, then make sure they give the right impression. If you would like some photos, then either ensure children's faces are not visible (in a natural way, not by blanking them out) or that you have permission from parents for this use.

ready to add the child's name and a photo, and another 'cubby' joins the wall.

Ongoing communication and consultation

Partnership with each parent needs to include regular communication, because children continue to be the responsibility of their own family. You discuss issues that affect a child. Parents are fully included in key decisions about their child's life in your provision, such as toilet training or the best way forward over Gary's intense fear of the dark.

You share information when there are several options and parents need to make the final decision – being honest when you reach the limits of your expertise. You may offer advice on an issue like referral to another professional. However, you accept the parent's decision, even if you feel it is unwise to turn down speech and language therapy for Nina. You may look for ways to make this a more acceptable option in the near future.

Parents should be confident they can trust practitioners not to gossip, or to repeat out of turn. You commit to confidentiality, but not to keeping secrets. You need to be clear about what kind of circumstances mean you have to seek other advice, even to overrule a parent's clearly stated choice. Such situations would usually be those when you had good reason to fear that the child is at temporary or longer term risk. Professional decisions are not always easy and you need to be able to discuss: between a key

person and the back up person, within room meetings and for a childminder to be able to discuss issues in a network meeting or with the childminding coordinator.

Example from a setting

As the EYFS makes clear, close relationships are equally important in both group provision and within the childminding service. The following issues arose from my conversations with members of the Charlton Childminding Network:

- **Conversational feedback to childminders, as well as a local questionnaire, had highlighted that what parents most wanted that for their baby or child was was that it was loved and had an enjoyable day. This focus on nurture was a greater priority than concerns about 'stimulating activities', or the EYFS in particular.**

- **Childminders offered a professional service which could be flexible to families, but nevertheless needed to keep some clear boundaries. The challenge was to be clear about non-negotiable professional obligations, such as safeguarding, so that this confidence could underpin what could come across to parents as a relatively informal approach.**

- **The childminders had a settling-in period for all children and a written agreement with each family. It was as important, as for group settings, that childminders were clear about the limits to their service and their expectations, such as payment of the agreed fees. In fact, some childminders said that money could be the most sensitive issue to manage in their practice.**

- **Some issues were genuinely open to discussion and, as should be the situation for every key person, the childminders paid attention to creating**

Links to your practice

It is worth reflecting on the content of your regular conversations with parents.

- The main aim is to share highlights of a baby or child's day. You communicate what the baby or toddler would say, 'If I had the words'.

- Avoid an imbalance towards what has gone wrong, especially very minor altercations between children that were fully resolved at the time.

- However, you need to be honest with parents about their own child and problems that do need your joint attention.

In some provision, it is possible to have a conversation with each parent, because they arrive and leave at staggered times. You need to resolve the practical issues of a setting where parents all arrive at around the same time.

- Do you ensure that over the week, each key person has at least a brief conversation with individual parents of every key child?

continuity with the child's home routines, as much as possible. However, it was not responsible to offer to be consistent with unhealthy eating patterns and childminders needed to find ways to talk with parents about this issue.

- Childminders needed to feel confident in their own practice, so that they can explain what they do and why to parents – both those who are considering their service and parents whose children already attend.

- Childminders sometimes developed close and long-term relationships with parents who might feel more comfortable confiding in their childminder than in far less familiar social care or health professionals.

In the Charlton area, as elsewhere, some childminders had undergone further training and were able to take referrals from social care services for vulnerable families. Even young children have often been through serious upheavals and a sequence of changes.

- Childminders in this position offer a close relationship through times of trouble to parents or other family members who have stepped into the parental role. The professional role can be to offer reassurance and close links with other support services.

- But sometimes the family carers feel isolated and they just want to chat with a fellow adult about the ordinary stuff of life when you care for young children. Conversations are not always complex or about highly sensitive issues.

You have ground rules that apply to everyone who comes to your home as a childminder or into your group setting. It is important to explain the do's and any don'ts to parents and other family members, without sounding like a nag or as if you are expecting trouble.

- If you have a phrase like: 'This is a no-smoking zone', is it clear that you mean the whole site and not only indoors?

- Do you have a written notice like: 'This is a no shouting, no smacking area'? How do you explain the reasons for this 'don't'?

- What will parents make of a phrase like: 'Racist or sexist language and behaviour will not be tolerated in our playgroup'? Will they know what you mean? Can you rephrase better it through the 'do' rule of courtesy to all?

Think twice before you simply pin up a notice that has come from elsewhere. Maybe your authority has issued a flier in response to some local incidents of verbal and physical abuse from parents. Is the wording compatible with the spirit of partnership or is it confrontational? How is this notice likely to affect those parents, whose reactions can be disruptive? And those parents who have never take an aggressive line?

Inclusion and partnership

You have a continuing obligation to deal with all the parents in an equal way. There will be differences between you and individual parents and some sources of diversity may feel like a wide gap. Professional practice is to recognise and deal with feelings that may block partnership. Effective partnership working recognises that some families may feel more or less at ease and responsible practitioners will explore how that might have arisen.

If you work in a diverse neighbourhood then there will be parents with whom you do not share the same ethnic identity, cultural background, language or faith. You need to approach all parents in an even-handed way. It would be poor practice to develop a closer partnership with parents who happen to share your own ethnic group, cultural background or faith. The obligation to behave in an even-handed way applies to everyone.

Fellow adults can be talking the same language with equal confidence and still feel that they are at cross purposes. However, personal communication becomes less straightforward when you do not share a language to the same level of fluency. It will usually help if you:

- Keep your words simple and sentences short. You do not have to sound patronising; it shows respect to enable the other person to process what you have said and have time to reply.

- Perhaps another family member or a friend can ease the conversation. In that case, you need to look at and talk to the parent, as well as including the 'translator' in your eye contact.

- Ensure that you are not left out of a lengthy exchange that you cannot understand and so cannot share important comments. Ask: "Please bring me back into the conversation".

- Aim to produce the most important written material in the main family languages that are spoken in your neighbourhood. Local services may help you with this, or you may be fortunate that a team member or parent can help. Stay part of this process and talk about the meaning of English words or phrases that do not easily translate.

Links to your practice

Part of good communication is to set up the expectation that parents will raise queries in a timely way and not let concerns fester. Early years practitioners need to set a good example by doing the same.

- It is a fair expectation that parents should talk first with their childminder or the key person in a group setting and not go straight to someone else as the first step in a difference of opinion.

- Relations will not always be plain sailing and in times of disagreement or outright complaint, practitioners deserve support within their own team and for childminders from the local childminding support worker.

- You should keep good quality records because a daily diary or other updates are part of sharing children's learning with the family. However, timely recording can also be helpful to support your stance that you did mention that incident or raise that health concern.

- In the same way as you should for putting children at their ease, aim to learn some phrases in the family language, at least greetings or thanks.

Some parents will have children with disabilities; some parents will themselves have a disability. Good practice in partnership recognises likely individual needs – perhaps a competent signer to support this conversation about the move into helping Becky with toilet training. However, it would be poor practice to assume in advance that a disabled parent will be unable to follow suggestions for coping with problems around bedtime routine with an exhausted child. You have a conversation about possibilities, and what this parent believes could work in her or his own family.

Another possibility is that a parent has a disability that affects communication, for instance, deafness or a stutter. However, practitioners may themselves live with hearing loss or disfluency in their speech.

- If you are deaf or have one 'good side', then it is important to tell parents and children. Otherwise, they may think you are inattentive or disinterested.

- If a parent is deaf, then you need to face the person, talk at normal volume and speak clearly, without your hand in front of your mouth – an unconscious habit of some people.

- Do not raise your voice; shouting distorts any sounds that can be heard and the process of interpreting lip and mouth movements.

- Some parents have a stutter that interrupts the fluency of their speech. This difficulty usually becomes worse when people feel rushed. You will help by avoiding any body language messages of being short of time. Do not finish parents' sentences for them; it is experienced as discourteous and you will often be wrong.

- A parent with a hearing or speech disability may find communication easier through a hearing friend. This three-way conversation needs the same care as when you do not speak the same language: share your attention between the parent and the friend.

Does 'parents' mean fathers too?

It is poor practice to treat fathers differently from mothers. For instance, if you wanted to discuss the recent changes in Ciaran's behaviour, you should not postpone that conversation until a day when his mother picks up her son. Nor should you assume that a father – as a lone parent or part of a couple – will be tougher on discipline.

Some early years teams judge the involvement of fathers by their presence in special activities or events. However, Ciaran's father is unlikely to become engaged in any other way, unless he already feels part of a friendly working relationship with his child's early years provision. So, as with mothers, the first and continuing strand of good practice in partnership has to be a positive relationship. It seems that some fathers do feel intimidated by early years practitioners (but so do some mothers). However, many fathers also speak of feeling welcomed and able to engage with their child's nursery or pre-school.

A great deal depends on the behaviour of early years practitioners, led by their child's key person in a group setting. The professional approach is to ensure that you offer as warm a welcome to a child's father, as you should to the mother. It is professional to address any 'personal baggage' of practitioners that risks disrupting relations with fathers. This appropriate phrase was chosen by the joint team from the University of Derby and the Pre-school Learning Alliance (Saunders et al. 2009).

- Good practice often has to start with discussion within the team: to unpick their expectations and assumptions. Be willing to reflect about whether, and why, James (father to Marie and her baby sister Sasha) does not receive equivalent attention to their mother.

- Does James seem to be very quiet? Then keep trying, and be welcoming. It is appropriate to add: 'Nice to see you again' for any parent whose presence is less regular. It is important that Marie's key person goes across to chat with James and share highlights of Marie's day.

- Perhaps Marie's mother, who usually does the pick-up, tends to dominate any conversation, even when James is standing there.

Links with your practice

You need to respect the way this family organises itself, but within that pattern you commit to making a positive relationship with both parents in two-parent households.

- Make the effort to invite both parents by name in any written invitation to open days or evenings.

- Some parents no longer live together. Unless there is a very good reason not to, then get contact details so you can invite the non-resident parent – often, but not always, the father.

- If both parents are present at daily drop-off or pick-up, or attend a meeting about their child then talk with them as equally as you can, even if one parent says more in the conversation than the other.

Be ready with a warm 'Hello' to James and respond to any interest, like, 'I saw you looking at the photos of our gardening project. We can always do with another pair of hands'.

- It is important not to make assumptions about 'all men' – or everyone in any kind of social grouping. But some projects have found that fathers, and other male family members, are more likely to respond to a definite, practical request than to non-specific invitations of, 'we welcome any kind of help'.

- The relationship may inevitably be different when one parent has become more familiar than the other. However, avoid assuming that fathers always have to rush off to work when they drop-off their children. You can ask: "Have you got a moment for Marie to show you…?"

- If you sense that a father (or a less familiar mother) is not at ease with the routine, then you can discreetly involve the child. For instance, you might suggest to Marie, 'Could you show Daddy where we keep the … ', or say directly to James, 'Sasha's nappies go in that blue bag over there. Thanks.'

- Perhaps James is very good looking and some team members risk getting their wires crossed? Recognise this issue – in the team, not with James – and work on putting his appearance to one side; treat him as Dad to Marie and Sasha. A team leader needs to address the situation, if any practitioner risks getting flirtatious with male family members.

- Some men (not all) are wary that their own friendliness will be misinterpreted. Perhaps James feels he got 'funny looks' when he joined a conversation with two mothers the first time he dropped off his daughters.

Sometimes practitioners focus on what makes some parents 'easier' to approach and this reflection can focus on mothers as well as fathers. It may be useful to understand better what leads you to feel more at ease. But, of course, the professional next step is to explore what you – not the parents – can do to improve communication and develop a positive relationship with every parent. Perhaps you feel it is easier to talk with Piya's father because he is that bit older and comes across as confident. Perhaps this aspect helped to launch good relations. But the professional responsibility is to fill that confidence gap from your side, if another parent appears to be waiting for you to make the first move.

Helping to make connections

Early years practitioners cannot, and should not try to, operate in isolation from the family of a baby or young child. Nor should they overlook other professionals, or places involved in the daily life of this child. The EYFS continues to recognise two broad ways in which the framework for partnership working encompasses how professionals work together for the well-being of families and children.

- Over early childhood, young children can be the responsibility of different early years practitioners, sometimes during the same period of time. You are responsible for ensuring continuity by sharing relevant information with other settings which the child attends.

- Some families are involved with a range of professionals in addition to the early years workforce. The EYFS is equally clear that practitioners need to work closely with professionals from other agencies involved with this family or child.

- Parents need to be aware that you communicate with other professionals and to be part of that process.

Early years practitioners would not make referrals without consultation with and the permission of parents. Partnership under these circumstances is all about an ongoing discussion, so your concerns do not come out of the blue. Parents need the chance to think over what you have said, or maybe add their own worries.

The exception is when child protection has become an issue, in which case you have no choice but to make a referral to social care services, if you are seriously concerned about a child. (This area of practice is fully covered in Lindon, 2012e.)

Example from a setting

Petts Wood Playgroup (PWPG) caters for children with a wide range of special needs. Families, with whom I spoke, appreciated the ease of conversation: that it was straightforward to hear about their child's day at pick-up time.

- **Parents felt that their child was treated as an individual. This respect was especially important, because some parents had experienced other professionals who approached their child as a problem or through a diagnosis.**

- **Throughout the term it is easy for parents to see photos that have been taken of children in their play. However, the termly open meeting for parents is a chance to see further displays of photos, for instance of special trips with the children. In the meeting,**

Food for thought

Partnership for families includes the working relationships with other agencies. Sometimes this contact is because another professional wishes to make a referral to your service. Anna Batty of Millom Children's Centre pointed out that you need to know what that other professional has said to the family, if anything.

Your aim is to make a bridge between a family, who may need help or is isolated, and what the centre could offer. An initial visit to the family home will not create a good beginning to the relationship, if parents are uncertain, or have been miscued, about the reason for your arrival. Sometimes, it is crucial to know the exact words that have been said to the family, in order to manage expectations in a fair and accurate way. Anna Batty described it as: "You need to know why the family think you are here."

In what ways does this insight apply to your own work in partnership?

Early years practitioners should have a sound knowledge of child development. Parents are often aware that something is awry in their child's language or social reactions. On the other hand, you may be the first person to feel that all is not well.

Any concerns about hearing or vision need to be expressed, since local health facilities do not automatically invite parents to bring their young child for developmental checks, including basic checks like hearing.

same roof as the early years provision for the children. Many larger settings, whatever their precise name, had been working according to this principle for some time: that it was helpful for families to be able to access relevant services and activities within a familiar place.

Example from a setting

I visited Windham Nursery School in 2004 when it was part of the Early Excellence initiative called Windham – A Partnership for Children. The aim was that a range of services could operate from the same building.

- **In Windham at that time, children from three to five years attended the nursery school sessions and younger children were able to attend the regular drop-in sessions with their parents.**

- **A range of specialist professionals came to see children at the centre and were able to assess individual children, and in some cases run specialist groups.**

- **An outreach worker took play out into the local community. The aim was to reach individual families who currently were unlikely to come to the centre, and to visit the Travellers site in the area.**

- **A portage team based at the centre took this home-based approach to families whose children had special needs.**

- **A toy library also operated from Windham, as well as a specialist team offering play sessions for school-age children with disabilities.**

- **A counselling service for children and adults was available, as well as a Helpline facility.**

Pound Park Nursery School in the London Borough of Greenwich developed another unit for the under threes in 2004 and joined with Sure Start Charlton in 2006 to become a Children's Centre. They run services in partnership with other agencies to meet the needs of local families.

where I was made welcome, a video was running, which included footage of all the children in recent special outings as well as play within the group.

A chance to talk and ask questions is especially valuable for parents of children with a disability or complex health needs.

- Some parents talked of the unclear communication with some (not all) professionals who have been involved in assessment of their child. It had been a relief to know that unanswered questions, and possible confusion, could be raised in the playgroup. They were confident of getting an explanation and a straight answer.

- PWPG has been organised with the aim of bringing services to the centre itself and using the rooms that are available. Parents were pleased to be able to see a range of professionals in a familiar environment – familiar for their child as well as for them. PWPG is supported by regular visits from a physiotherapist, occupational therapist, speech and language therapist, educational psychologist and a paediatrician.

- It has been helpful for some families to have information about services or resources for which they can apply, as a parent of a child with special needs. Support is also welcome for when a child is going through the process of assessment for a statement of special educational needs.

One of the key aims for the Children's Centre initiative in England was to bring together a range of services for families under the

- The Children's Centre has a large Family Room which has two spaces: one room suitable for meetings and workshops or courses, and a second room which operates more as a playroom and has outdoor space as well.

- The local childminding network meets here on a weekly basis.

- A range of workshops and courses are run for parents and other family members. For example, a baby massage session runs that is open to any parents from the neighbourhood.

- The local midwife runs a drop-in on one morning a week.

- The walls of the Family Room are also used to provide information about local services and raise awareness about issues such as domestic violence.

- A counselling service also operates from this part of the centre.

The other crucial aspect to partnership is that practitioners need to ease the transition of children and families from one form of provision to another. The experience of transition is supported through a considerate ending of one working relationship and the beginning of another. But it is equally important that teams stretch out to each other and build that bridge for young children and their families.

Example from a setting

In Sun Hill Infants School, the reception class team works in close partnership with the local pre-schools, which children attend prior to coming to Sun Hill. The aim is to ease the transition for children and families. They have worked together for consistency on the children's record of achievement and to avoid over-assessing young children.

Care is taken to explain to families how Sun Hill operates, including that the team regard Year 1 as the gentle transition for children towards a more structured school approach. The experience of reception (which Sun Hill calls Year F) is play-based and strongly led by children's expressed interests. The team take a developmentally realistic approach to the literacy skills of young children, and offer support when those skills are genuinely delayed.

Different kinds of involvement

This section explores different ways in which parents and other family carers might be invited to be closely involved with their child's learning and experiences in early years provision. There is no set approach that will be right for everyone, because settings and the parents whose children attend will never be the same. For any given centre or childminder, the pattern is also likely to change over time as the result of turnover in the families who use your provision.

> ## Parents as partners in their child's learning

The core to partnership has to be open communication in terms of regular conversation and use of personal records of children, with reports like a daily diary that often travel between the family home and nursery or the childminder's home.

Example from a setting
You share highlights of the day in conversation with a mother or father. But parents and children alike really appreciate something more permanent.

- **Georgina Mellish-Laws, a childminder from south London, is very committed to getting children outdoors and is part of the local Forest School initiative. She described two special books in which she documented children's experiences in their Forest School sessions, but also the highlights of their regular walks in the local park.**

Words matter but, in any early years provision, photos can be a powerful message about what engaged a child today and this week.

- **Buckingham's Nursery School has a laptop set up in the open reception area, providing a slide show of photos from this week. I have talked with childminders who have taken the same opportunity in their home.**

- **I have seen dedicated shelves for work in progress, with a child's name card against their project that may not be finished today. Southlands Kindergarten, like some other day nurseries I have visited, has cleared a low shelf for children to place anything they wish to show their parent(s) at pick-up time.**

> ## Food for thought
>
> Childminders in the Charlton Childminding Network raised the sensitive issue of what to do/say about significant developmental milestones. I have had similar conversations with practitioners in day nurseries. Do you tell a parent that their toddler took their first step today or appeared to say a real word?
>
> Experienced practitioners recognise how much time the children of working parents can spend in the care of their childminder or key person. You will be excited when your key baby or toddler does something new. However, it is considerate to wait until a parent shares an important milestone from home. You could contribute, 'she's so close to ...' or 'It won't be long before he ...'.
>
> When you have established an easy two-way communication, then mothers and fathers will tell you about magic moments from family life. They are confident that you are interested.
>
> Such conversations can also be your opportunity to put an event in context. For instance, what Marie has brought in from home is a good example of emergent writing and is in no way 'just scribble'. You contribute to this exchange with your care in building up each child's individual portfolio, to show an individual learning journey.

- It is important that practitioners do not tidy up as a matter of course towards the end of the day. Some child-initiated projects and large scale constructions need to be viewed in their place – perhaps out in the garden. Some important projects can be left overnight.

- In Sun Hill reception class, it was possible for two girls to leave their blocks construction, with their names and a work in progress sign. It was possible for their parents to see their ongoing work. But it was also understood that the school cleaners would not disturb the work.

As well as personal conversations with parents you can use other channels for sharing with families what you do and why. You can use the potential of wall displays or large-scale (A3 size) information books. For either format, think about the main messages you want to get across to parents or other visitors. Similar points apply to what you include in a child's personal book or portfolio.

- Let well-chosen photos speak for you. Think about why you picked this photo, what does it say? Think about a short caption. It often works well to have the child(ren) in the image to do the 'speaking'. So write phrases from the children's perspective, and reflect this by using the pronouns 'I' or 'we'.

- Think about what else you write. In general, it is better to avoid phrases like, 'we enjoy painting', because 'like' or 'enjoy' is pretty much a given. You would not display a photo with, 'I hate sand but they make me play in it'.

- Look at the child(ren)'s face(s) and recall (or check your notes for) what they said during the time they were fully engaged in this experience. Did they spend ages working out how to build this castle? Did this small group have a lively discussion about …?

- Only use quotation marks ("…") when these enclose what children really said, or put their words in a speech bubble. If you cannot recall the exact phrase, then choose your short sentences to be as close as possible.

- Think twice before you simply copy in words from your early years guidance. What sense will this heading make to parents? Is this quoted phrase the best way to convey your message?

- Avoid being in a hurry to complete a wall display or large book. A steady build-up communicates the valuable message that learning grows over time, takes unexpected turns and is often much more about the excitement of the journey than what we made, if anything, by the end.

- I have seen excellent displays that showed: 'We're finding out about …', 'this week we learned that …' and 'now we want to know about …'. Group settings have had 'Our Big Question for this week is …' and documented with children the shared learning story of 'How we made our herb garden'.

Example from a setting

There is a great deal of visual information easily available in the entrance area for the Pound Park Children's Centre.

- **A table has several A3 size books that show different aspects of early learning. Well-chosen photos and**

Links to your practice

Regular communication with parents needs to be supported by regular, slightly more formal times to have a lengthier conversation about individual children. You need to work out the best way to organise this opportunity.

Pound Park Children's Centre moved to an Open Week system, once a term. This event is a whole week during which parents are invited to sign up for a time that is convenient to them to come in to talk with their child's key person in detail about progress and sensible next steps in early learning. The centre has found the Open Week option works better for most families than a single open evening. However, parents who cannot organise to come during any of the days are welcome to make an evening appointment.

How do you organise this kind of communication?

straightforward explanatory text bring alive each area of learning and development of the EYFS.

- **A large wall display about writing gives the clear message that this skill takes time to development and children learn gradually. Photos and examples show the important mark making done by enthusiastic young children and what emergent writing looks like.**

- **Practical tips explain what will genuinely help young girls and boys. The details show, as well as tell, the message that writing can take place anywhere, so long as children have the tools and their own motivation for wanting to record in different ways.**

Good two-way communication can enable you to offer information about your overall plans for the next few weeks and invite families to join in the development of this theme or project.

Some displays may be part of a specific aim to communicate with parents about developmentally appropriate practice. For instance, you can support parents' understanding of a genuine build-up of early literacy skills when you share the details of this particular learning journey.

- Consider displays that use actual events and photos from your time with children and organise them under a heading like: 'When I'm older, I'll be ready to learn how to write, because now I am busy learning about ...'.

- You then have photos, with appropriate captions, that show young children making their own marks in many different ways, using different mark-making tools or happily carrying around their own clipboard. You might have an image of children gathered around an adult writing for a purpose, with the explanation: 'We helped Andy write all our good ideas about ...'.

- You could do a similar display about the steps towards reading, which could include photos and captions that show, and explain, 'I have my favourite books', 'We have made up our own story about the scary forest', 'We know so many rhymes' or 'Did you know this sign tells us the way to the library'.

- The same pattern could be followed to document this important process in an A4 booklet style, left available for parents or children to browse. Some group settings cannot fix anything to the wall of their shared building. Childminders and small nurseries may have limited available wall space.

Example from a setting
In Sun Hill reception class the team's approach to topics is very flexible and each broad area starts with direct involvement of families.

I visited towards the end of a summer term, when the topic was transport. Like every other line of exploration,

this topic started with an A4 sheet sent home with a brief explanation of the topic and the invitation that parents talk with their child and reach a question that this child wants to investigate. Parents wrote the question on the sheet and sometimes children had illustrated their thought-provoking queries.

Some examples were: 'How do you drive a motor bike?', 'How many different types of boat are there?', 'Why do trains go on tracks?' and 'How do underwater trains move – like the one that goes to France?'. A full wall had been filled with the sheets and anyone could become involved in this investigation. Lines of enquiry and findings steadily joined the display – very detailed by this point in the term.

The walls of Sun Hill Infants School included several large displays that documented projects that had been undertaken with the children. One wall display about the Magical Musical Garden explained how children had been actively involved at every stage: in the ideas, design and making of the outdoor facility. As well as showing the process visually, this display also explained for families how children and their teachers had taken a problem solving approach that included reflection, generation of ideas and evaluation.

Some group settings plan an event, where the main objective is to share more general information about children's experiences here.

- Several teams have described to me a successful event in which they have set up the nursery or playgroup ready for play. Parents and other family adults come along on a Saturday or other time that suits family life and get their hands on the resources, sometimes without their children. Some, if not all, team members are available to talk with parents, add the information about what their children do and to make the connections between this kind of resource or experience and how it supports early learning.

- You may organise an information session or evening about some aspect of early learning. You need to be sure, from discussion with parents, that they would welcome this focus. Perhaps it has been raised as a direct request or your suggestion has been met with genuine enthusiasm. Ideally, this session will be run by the team. If you judge it is valuable to bring in an outside speaker, then make sure this person will connect their contribution closely with what happens in your setting.

You may decide to show visual material in an information session that you and your colleagues run.

- If you are using photos in a slide show, then think about why you have chosen these images. What do they communicate for you? What do you need to add?

- Do a dry run to check how long your presentation will take. Have you got too many images, such that you have to go at a breakneck speed?

It is worth thinking over the practical issues for any invited event.

■ Be clear about the aim of this event, promote it in good time and think about your use of words. Have you removed specialist early years phrases, which are not necessarily obvious to other adults?

■ Plan your timing by finding out what will work best for the parents whose children currently attend. If you plan an evening event, can parents bring their children or will there be a crèche? Some families may have nobody to sit with the children at home, or cannot afford to pay a sitter.

■ Basic hospitality is welcome, if only hot and cold drinks, If you offer snacks, then make sure there are clearly labelled vegetarian options – handy also for anyone who needs their meat or poultry prepared in a given way.

■ It is useful to get an idea of who is likely to attend. You may decide to go ahead, even if the anticipated numbers are low. Any photos or displays you organise may well then transfer to the wall or into a ring binder file that will be available for anyone to see.

Sharing ideas with parents

Another approach has been to create opportunities to share ideas with parents about resources and suitable experiences for their baby or child. Some ideas have been developed in settings, arising from one-off trial events like the open session for parents to play. Other initiatives have developed because of requests from parents for more information about resources that they know their children enjoy. Three large scale projects offer a good source of ideas:

■ The Peers Early Education Partnership (PEEP) programme, based in Oxford, has a long track record in creating a workshop format and appropriate supporting materials to encourage and enable parents to be active in their child's early learning. They have a strong focus on engaging parents about their feelings and talking over why something works well. There is also an enduring theme of building confidence and self-esteem for parents, as well as their children (www.peep.org.uk).

■ The PEAL project (Parents, Early Years and Learning) was based from 2005-7 at the Early Childhood Unit of the National Children's Bureau. Funded by the DfES (now the DCSF), the project offers training but has also brought together case studies of different ways that early years centres have successfully created a connection between home and early years provision (www.peal.org.uk).

■ Do you intend to use sequences filmed in your setting? Despite the greater simplicity of the technology now, making a film still takes a lot of time. Avoid this option unless you can ensure good quality – not something that will provoke nervous laughter from the team or 'sorry you can't hear it properly'.

■ You may consider using excerpts of DVD from materials you have bought. Again, be sure what job you want this sequence to do. You will hand over control to another medium and you cannot comment while it is running.

■ It should go without saying, that you have already watched the visual material fully at least once. Line up a video to the section you want and have a clear note for the section you want in a DVD unless you have it poised to go.

■ If there is something you especially want parents to notice then say so in advance. But do not talk too long about what is coming.

■ Consider the length of the sequence. You probably need at least three minutes, or else the excerpt is too short. If you get much longer than ten minutes in one go, there may be too much information for clarity in later discussion.

- The Parents as Partners in Early Learning project (PPEL) was funded by the government to explore innovative ways of working with families, especially vulnerable parents, to encourage their involvement in their children's development and early learning. (You can read ten case studies at www. dcsf.gov.uk. http://www.education.gov.uk/publications/ standard/publicationDetail/Page1/DfES/1081/2004)

Developing this aspect of partnership needs all the careful thought that has been discussed so far. The good ideas on the above websites cannot, of course, simply be airlifted into any setting without consideration of local issues and priorities. However, case studies are valuable for starting ideas running and as food for thought about possible issues. For instance:

- One PPEL project explored ways to engage fathers in active play. The approach was successful, partly because the practitioners identified early on that some fathers were ill-at-ease, thinking they could somehow fail. The activities were genuinely open-ended and other fathers ceased to worry about a right or wrong option, once one father had taken the plunge and developed a game.

- The PEAL website describes two projects in which parents made Story Sacks: the collection of items that appear in a storybook and which can then be used as props for bringing the book alive in a story telling way. I have encountered other settings who are happy to lend to families from a store of Story Sacks.

- Chris Athey's (1990) research with the play patterns of schemas was a project all about parent involvement. And continued by some early years teams, notably by Pen Green Centre in Corby. (You can get a sense of the approach from part of the workbook used with parents and childminders at www.leics.gov.uk/penn_green_schemas.pdf).

Example from a setting

The World of Discovery project in Thurrock, led by Debbie Shepherd, was established with funding from PPEL. Several small projects were undertaken, one of which was the World of Discovery initiative. This project was facilitated by Ellie Reynish, a community artist. The aim was to introduce very young children to a variety of materials that they could explore in an open-ended way. As the session evolved, other resources were introduced, but on the basis of what had interested babies and toddlers. The linked aim was to show parents, who were always present, that it was possible to engage young children with resources that cost very little to buy, such as small amounts of material like organza or net curtaining, a large rectangle of cellophane, simple bowls and short lengths of small link chain.

As the idea spread out from the first early years centre, Debbie Shepherd ensured that she bought any resources for subsequent projects within the local neighbourhood.

So, it was really possible for her to say – to parents, and early years practitioners who became very interested – that 'you can get any of this yourself'. No items are expensive. Just like the Treasure Basket or Heuristic Play approach, it is important that the responsible adult checks all the resources so that items are replaced as soon as they look worn-out. Materials need to be stored in a way that keeps them in good condition and makes it easy to find resources around a common theme.

It was important to allow this kind of project time to get established. A taster session initially attracted a very small turnout. However, more and more parents hear about the session, came and liked it. The session had to be divided into two because of the turnout of parents – fathers as well as mothers – and some grandparents. Another practical issue was to recognise that parents took time to become accustomed to the sensory materials and that they were never toys in the conventional sense.

It was important to be clear about the adult role: that is was fine for the baby or toddler to get hold of the materials and treat them in unexpected ways. The development worker

---

Links to your practice

A range of good ideas to link home and early years provision are already well established in some settings.

- I have encountered different versions of a special soft toy that goes home at weekends with an individual child. Teddy (or whoever) takes part in the ordinary events with the family. Parents are welcome to complete a diary and/or take photos. Teddy's account grows over time and is a source of conversation.

- Children are often keen to borrow favourite books or toys from nursery. Some teams have made the decision to create a lending system.

- One practitioner described (in one of my training days) how they had created a card system for lending books. Children understood the simple writing or visuals. So they were able to take an active role in finding the relevant card and giving instructions about how their name should be written down.

- Another nursery had organised some simple bags with the nursery logo. 'Officially' borrowed resources travelled to and from family homes in the bag.

What have you done in your setting to 'formalise' children's wish to borrow? How do you respect the flipside – that children often really want to bring in important items or toys from their home? They want to make this connection.

in any session would explain and model that the role of the adult was to be close, show their interest and help if it was obvious that a baby or toddlers wanted some assistance. The development worker also modelled commenting briefly about what a baby or toddler was doing, often to the parent. These relevant comments also helped to attune parents to all the little, yet important, aspects of how very young children explore their world.

In each 'Discovery' session the materials have a common feature, yet remain varied. So, the focus can be shiny and reflective materials, texture, sound, materials that envelop a baby and young child or which vary in smell. The aim is also that some resources can be hung, some are spread on the floor, where babies are sitting or lying on a comfortable surface (adults are also on the floor) and that it is possible for babies and toddlers to do something with most of the resources, as well as look at them or listen. They can definitely get their hands onto the materials.

Ellie Reynish took photos of the babies and children fully involved in their explorations. The images, with simple explanations, were available for parents to see. The project also offered handouts for parents with suggestions of what they could do to continue this kind of learning at home. Each parent then had their own illustrated book to keep at the end of the run of sessions. Similar books, full of images and brief written explanations, are made available in the entrance area of any centre where such sessions run.

This approach has proved successful in showing parents how much babies and really young children gain from simple materials. Parents who attended on a regular basis were able to talk about what their baby had gained and share that personal learning journey with other parents who had come new to the experience. The project has continued in several children's centres and has a portfolio of images that show how the open-ended sessions engage children, plus a wide range of back up sheets that list the kind of materials that work well.

Sometimes teams have considered how to bring parents on board with significant projects.

Example from a setting

The Greenwich Forest School Project has successfully developed a range of projects across this area of south London and provides a good example of how the Forest School approach can definitely work in an urban area. A key strand in the success of this project has been the commitment to involve and inform parents from the earliest stages.

One such project operates out of Pound Park Children's Centre and had developed a local outdoor space called Gilbert's Pit, which is very close to the centre. Partnership with families is an essential part of this kind of development. I was able to hear about the practical issues from Liz Danks, the Pound Park Forest School Leader, Alexa Gilbert, who runs the under threes unit, and two highly involved childminders, Carole Allen and Ellen Edwards.

- Some parents – not all – were wary about their children being outdoors in general and a 'wild' space in particular. Practitioners took care to explain what would happen, to reassure them about safety, deal with suitable clothing and getting dirty, muddy or cold and practical issues like going to the toilet.

- Some parents in different projects across Greenwich were able to relate their own outdoor interests to what was now on offer for their young children. Some recalled, with nostalgia, how much they had enjoyed the outdoors in their own childhood. Other parents needed to get used to the idea.

- The key practitioners at Pound Park organised a Parents' barbecue in Gilbert's Pit at the outset of the project. It was a great advantage that families could see the area and hear about what was planned.

Conversations continued to reassure anyone about aspects of safety. Some of these parents then became involved in helping to clear the site. A lot of hard physical work was necessary to get the area ready for children.

- Family members are always welcome to join their children in the weekly visit to the forest and additional help is necessary to meet the adult-child ratio when children are taken anywhere outside the Children's Centre. About three parents come on a regular basis and others, including some grandparents, come on an occasional basis.

- Many parents are working, so shared experiences need to be offered at the weekend. Two Saturday sessions gave all family members a direct experience of the activities that their children enjoyed. One of several Dads' Brunch events was specifically about the Forest Schools and offered a chance to visit the site on that day.

- Children were quickly enthusiastic and their feedback helped the more cautious parents to take a positive view. The centre has been getting feedback from parents who have adapted their own garden to enable children to get involved outdoors. The team ensure that children's individual profile books include examples and photos from their Forest School experiences.

- I heard examples of young children, even under twos, who took their enthusiasm over Forest School with their childminder into time with their own family. One 18-month-old boy had shown his parents his skills in clambering and balancing. A two year old girl had been able to show her family that she could carry sticks safely. Conversations between their childminder and parents filled the gap over experiences that very young children could not yet put into spoken words.

General support and help from families

Some patterns of active involvement focus on support from parents for activities within the setting or extended services of a large centre. For instance, you may make a request for play materials such as dressing up clothes, loads of corks or cardboard tubes. It is sensible to explain briefly why you would welcome these materials. If your request is for further supplies, put some photos on the wall or board for parents, showing children's enjoyment so far with these resources.

Example from a setting
In The Grove Nursery School the children themselves were directly involved in requests to parents for useful resources. On the day of my visit I watched as several children, working with a practitioner, planned the details of an A4 sheet that would ask parents for materials to source the children's planned role play area, which was to be a hairdressing salon. The children were busy in discussion about what they needed and what families might be able to give. They organised illustrations, agreed on what the practitioner should write and then photocopied their final draft. The children were ready with their sheets and they gave one to each parent at pick-up time.

Food for thought

Any setting has to consider their approach to partnership in light of their local community. Millom Children's Centre serves a small town, which is geographically isolated and with some families living in the surrounding countryside with no car.

- Anna Batty focused on the need to keep any programme realistic. If a centre is tempted to be over-ambitious, then some events may be less suitable or have not benefited from enough prior thought and planning.

- Supporting local families, let alone bringing about positive change, is not a quick fix. Progress is often a slow burn – for the reflective practice of teams as well as the pace of learning and comfort for parents.

- The Millom team has reflected on the importance of telling parents what they cannot do, and the reasons. A culture of honesty includes a commitment not to make promises that cannot be fulfilled.

- Three key questions guide the Millom team: Why are we doing this? Who are we doing it for? So what? You might like to think of how you answer these deceptively simple questions.

Another strand of partnership is to ask parents to share their skills and time. Depending on the nature of your early years provision, you may invite parents to become involved in fundraising activities.

- Some early years settings have limited predictable income and raising additional funds is part of the annual pattern. Parents may be really needed to help with organising sponsored walks and car boot sales or to provide food for fundraising tea parties or summer barbecues. These events may also be enjoyable social occasions for everyone.

- Nurseries, whose main income is from fees paid by parents, may still have annual events that fund what families understand to be extras – equipment or special outings. Parents who do not wish to be involved in any aspect of organisation may still enjoy attending a summer fun day or food from around the world event.

Another aspect of potential involvement is for parents to be present within the day or session that their child attends. Some early years provision could not operate without a rota of volunteers, who may (or may not) be parents of children currently attending the group. Parents may be welcome as occasional, but predictable, helpers within the daily activities of the group – perhaps to share personal skills such as woodwork or gardening. Some local outings or special trips may not be feasible without additional adults.

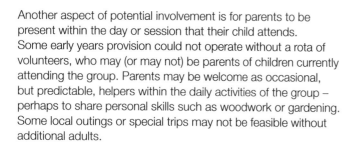

Food for thought

Some parents may be interested in becoming directly involved in your provision in one or more of the ways described in this section. On the other hand, some parents are very committed to their own child(ren), but are not in the position to spend time involved in their child's day with you. The whole point is that they need you to take full responsibility for those agreed hours. Mothers and fathers may be holding down a paid job, they may be students, they may want time with their other children, or they may simply want a short break.

It would be poor practice for any early years provision to judge parents' interest against their (un)willingness to be physically present in the nursery or take a regular turn on the playgroup rota. Any team that takes a narrow view of 'this is parent involvement' and 'they don't want to be involved' should take a big mental step back and reflect on creating a more two-way model of partnership.

Some patterns of possible involvement raise the question of whether parents will need to be vetted. The implementation of the Safeguarding Vulnerable Groups Act 2006 has changed the legal requirements to protect children in England and Wales. Similar legislation applies in Scotland and Northern Ireland. The new system came into force in September 2012. This section does not constitute legal advice. Readers are responsible for checking their situation on www.homeoffice.gov.uk/publications/crime/disclosure-and-barring.

The law now places more responsibility onto provision to make a considered judgement over whether the specific role of paid workers or volunteers necessitates their being vetted. If your provision is part of a larger body, then you need to find out the position that has been taken for anyone within the organisation.

In general, anyone providing what is called a 'regulated activity' for children (close contact) on a 'frequent' basis (once a month or more) or 'intensive' pattern (happening three or more days in a 30 day period) should be vetted. The checks ensure there is no reason to suppose they are unsafe to be in close contact with children. It is irrelevant whether individuals will be paid or not.

The vetting process – similar to the Criminal Records Bureau (CRB) checks – involves finding out whether this person has been involved in criminal activity which would mean they pose a risk to children. The new process will also cover whether serious questions have been raised about the person's behaviour in that context. These checks do not remove the broader professional obligations about safeguarding children (Lindon, 2012e). As with the previous system, the new vetting and barring rules can only identify people whose past behaviour has raised serious concerns.

Unless you are part of an organisation that has decided to take a stricter line, then it seems clear that you do not have to ask family members to go through the checking process, when they accept an occasional invitation to spend time in your setting. Maybe Hamid's mother is pleased to join you, talk with the children about Eid-al-Fitr and share some of her family's food. Likewise, no vetting is required for parents who join your yearly visit to the fire station or help out at fund-raising events.

However, suppose the Eid visit blossoms into a suggestion that Hamid's mother could offer a food preparation and cooking time every Tuesday. Another example would be that the weekly nursery trip to the local library cannot happen without the reliable support of Teja's grandmother and Michael's father. You, or your overall organisation, could decide that the family members will be fully supervised by (vetted) staff and so no further checks are required. However, you need to consider your judgement for any event would be classified as a regulated activity, if it were unsupervised.

Activities and events organised for parents

Some early years teams have developed a programme of events in response to requests from parents. I have encountered centres who have offered arts and crafts, cooking, English as an additional language and maths – to list only a few ideas. Some workshop experiences include suitable activities to share with young children. However, some are focused on what parents want to learn to boost their own confidence, but they do not feel ready to join local adult education classes. They are comfortable to attend sessions in a familiar early years centre.

As Liz Klavins (2008) points out, the leadership of Children's Centres can be under pressure from government funding to hit health targets over smoking or obesity. However, sound professional judgement is that an intervention will feel like nagging unless parents are motivated to tackle a specific topic. Teams need to reflect on how they approach important health issues.

There is considerable concern about the extent to which even young children are overweight, and even clinically obese. Early childhood is a crucial time to lay down healthy habits of enthusiasm for good quality food and drink, and also enjoyment of lively physical exercise through play. Some parents may ask you directly for advice, but your main approach will be to lead through the good example of your own practice.

- Let parents know through your weekly menu, as well as when talking to them, what their baby or child ate today.

- Some settings are unable to offer a midday meal to children and so families send in a packed lunch. It is responsible for a setting to provide friendly guidelines, even to ask that some items are not added, such as fizzy drinks or crisps.

- Children need plenty of physical activity, much of it outdoors. Again your good practice should demonstrate that it is not appropriate to put young children on exercise programmes.

Links to your practice

Many joint events can be documented so that families know the different ways in which they could become involved.

- The family news board can have a display of photos of different family members as well as practitioners, under the heading of: 'Thanks to everyone who helped paint the outside walls this weekend. The children can now start on their mural – watch this space!'.

- A different kind of display could be: 'Thanks to everyone who was generous with their time for the playgroup this term'. This wall chart also includes a look ahead with, 'Next term we are keen to find people who would help with/know how to/have ideas of where we could find…'.

- Your choice of photos communicates appreciation for the help. But it is also a visual message that different family members can, and have, been directly involved in the life of the group.

- As well as individual parents, perhaps you are able to thank 'Jed (Greta's 'big' brother) for installing the anti-virus software' or 'Dina (Tim's grandma) who knew which plants would grow in our shady corner'.

You provide time, space, appropriate play resources and children will get plenty of exercise.

- If a child is visually overweight, you need to talk with parents. Be sure of your information if you offer advice, including that you do not put children on a 'diet' in the way that many adults use the word. The best and safest approach is to shift a child's food to a more nutritious balance, including proper meals rather than non-stop snacking. Young children have plenty of growing to do and, with a healthy diet and exercise, their upwards growth will deal with the weight, unless there are other special health problems.

Example from a setting
Parents can be invited to join in meals – either regular lunchtime or special events.

Wendy Scott (2009) described the initiatives of the Ashbrow Children's Centre, part of the Infant and Nursery School site. Parents take up on the open invitation to come and eat lunch with their children, as well as attendance at what has become an annual Christmas lunch for family members.

Other nurseries have also been successful in offering invitations for families to join their children in special meals. I have encountered lively 'Cook and Taste' sessions with children. Nurseries have offered to share recipes of children's favourites and put up a wall display along the lines of, 'We like fruit (or vegetables) – this week we tried ...'. Some enthusiasm over food has led to cooking sessions with parents.

Do you have events exclusively for men?

Research and anecdotal evidence continues to highlight the reality that early years provision comes across as very female. I have heard and read about a wide range of events, sometimes organised for the weekend, which are promoted for fathers and other men in the family such as uncles, 'big' brothers and granddads.

Example from a setting
I visited Pound Park Children's Centre in the summer of 2009 and they had been running events specifically for Dads for a couple of years.

- Active inclusion of fathers starts with those families whose children attend the under threes unit. This team work on the assumption that men will be closely involved with their babies and toddlers. Fathers are asked about family information and their baby's life so far, on an equal basis with the mothers.

- Sheena Gilbey, the head of Pound Park Centre, noticed there was a strong contingent of fathers from the under threes unit when the centre first started their events for Dads.

- The team aims to get to know all family carers who bring or pick up the children, and are on first name terms with everyone.

- They have chosen to start letters home with, 'Dear Mums, Dads and Carers', because they realised that 'Parents' was not always taken to mean everyone.

The centre had run a range of special events for the whole family, such as Carnival Week and joint creative endeavours, like making a mosaic. They decided to start some Saturday events for fathers with their children, on the basis of the practical advice emerging from fatherhood research projects.

- The team had consistent feedback after the first events that fathers really appreciated these times to be with their children. The view was that, if mothers were present, there was a high chance they took over what was happening.

- The events have a regular turnout of at least 30 fathers with their children, and not always the same men. Fathers are welcome to continue to attend after their children have left the nursery school and some choose to do so.

- Promotion of each event is by an invitation created by the children themselves and taken home. The events work as a social occasion and often have a practical focus such as sports, science, arts or language and literacy.

- The centre has also had a 'Bring your Dad to nursery day'.

Parenting groups and programmes

Some early years centres and primary schools offer one or more regular groups for parents, or other family carers. Most groups offer a social side of contact with fellow-adults, but some also include a specific aim of offering support and the opportunity of advice. Some groups follow a planned content, for instance, workshops that explore aspects of parenting. Other groups meet on a regular basis, but the content is determined by what people want to raise today. A successful and lively parents' group looks deceptively easy to run. Yet there are many practicalities underlying the smooth organisation and it is essential to have a leader/facilitator who understands group work (see Lindon and Lindon, 2008).

Some parents will ask for advice from their child's key person about different aspects of parenting a young child. Some centres are set up especially to support vulnerable families, with parents who may

Links to your practice

Partnership with families has to rest on regular, face-to-face communication. However, other channels for sharing information support the personal approach. A family notice board can be useful, so long as a team member is responsible for keeping the contents up to date and avoiding a clutter of old notices and leaflets.

A regular newsletter can be an effective way to share information about general events, past and present, in your provision. You can produce a good quality simple newsletter with a word processing package and careful choice of different fonts and some colour. If you are familiar with a publishing software package, it is possible to create a professional layout, and to insert illustrations.

Look at a relatively simple format from Twechar Nursery Class, East Dunbartonshire www.twechar.e-dunbarton.sch.uk/_files/nursery_class_newsletter_june_09.pdf and a more ambitious approach from Smisby Day Nursery in Ashby de la Zouch (www.smisbydaynursery.co.uk/downloads_newsletters.htm).

feel particularly uncertain over their skills of parenting. However, some childminders are accredited (and have gone through relevant training) to offer a specialist service for families with additional social and childcare needs. Local schemes have included childminding places for young children with health needs or disability, or families under severe stress. Some childminders provide support to young adolescent mothers who appreciate friendly guidance over their own parenting, as well as the childcare that enables them to continue with their studies at school or college.

Example from a setting

The approach of the team of Thongsley Fields Nursery and Primary School is that what is outside the school will become part of school life because experiences travel in with children. The team aim for personal relationships with children as individuals and positive relations with their family, including clear communication with families about their child's nursery, and then school experience. Additionally, the head, Rachel Meyer, has worked in partnership with other agencies to offer more extensive family support within the school. Initiatives are developed steadily: in response to what parents say they would welcome and then based on an evaluation of how an event or session has gone.

- **A community room is available for parents and a range of sessions are offered. Some, such as a baby and toddler music session, focus on activities that work well with babies or young children. A toy library operates from the school.**

- **The team at Thongsley Fields has recognised that some parents are keen to learn, but past experience has made them unlikely to start with a local college. Sessions have been offered on adult skills such as literacy, numeracy, computer skills, and practical messages around healthy eating.**

- **Parents commit to the whole run of sessions for Family Talk or for the ten week Raising Children parenting programme, which gives time for parents to explore how their own childhood has affected their approach to parenting their own children. Some parents have chosen to repeat the full course, recognising that their hard work on reflection means they are now in a different position and ready to learn more about positive parenting.**

Centres or schools that are able to run parenting sessions or programmes usually invite mothers and fathers equally and also welcome couples who are able to attend together. Some fathers-only sessions have developed in response to men's preference to talk with fellow males.

Example from a setting

The Fatherhood Institute has developed an approach called 'Hit the Ground Crawling' – a wonderful title.

Links to your practice

No group should be started within an early years centre or school unless you can guarantee the appropriate amount of time and skilled attention.

- One person from the practitioner team, or the same family support worker, should take responsibility for a group, even one with mainly social aims.

- A fund-raising parents' group might meet sometimes without a practitioner, but there should be regular communication with the same team member. A familiar and predictable face shows that this group is valued, provides continuity and builds trust.

- If the group facilitator/leader has to leave, then the change needs to be warned and the transition handled with courtesy and at least one session of joint working.

- Sometimes an open parents' group becomes unwelcoming to any new members. It can also happen that an informal group effectively establishes territorial rights over the parents' room. It is easier to spot this development earlier, when a practitioner or family support worker is regularly in the parents' room and available for informal conversations. You may have to act deliberately to bring in and support other parents to break the exclusive clique.

A small number of sessions, sometimes just a one-off (if preferred by the fathers) are offered to men who are about to become a father or whose partner has recently had a baby. Sessions were trialled in 2008 in East Staffordshire Children's Centre in Burton-on-Trent.

A family or community worker facilitated the sessions, but the content is led by conversation, question and answer between the men themselves. A recurring message is that a fathers-only session typically runs differently from when their female partners are present. Expectant fathers welcome a chance to hear from other men about the impending birth and labour. Some participants also say that, when women are present, there is more chance that they take over any discussion.

A role in policy and decision-making

Parents should of course have the necessary information and opportunity to participate in decisions about their own child. However, they may also be offered some involvement in the broader running of a setting.

- Friendly regular conversation will be the informal route to hear what parents think and feel. Sometimes this option is complemented by a suggestions box – ideally you want signed suggestions. An alternative is to have a regular time, perhaps every quarter year, or end of term, if you work on a termly basis. Not all parents will be confident to write their comments, so you can offer to write down ideas in your own notebook.

- Some group settings invite family opinion on a regular basis via a short questionnaire, probably no more than two pages in length. You need to think about one or two topics on which you would welcome opinions. For example, perhaps three months ago you shifted to free flow between indoors and the garden. Or you have reorganised the pattern of children's individual portfolios. You can have a couple of open-ended questions about 'what has your child wanted to tell you about' or 'what has your child wanted to show you'?

- Open meetings for parents could allow them to express their views about the recent changes or future plans, for instance about steps towards healthier eating.

There is encouragement, sometimes even pressure, that children's centres should have a Parents Forum. But this approach does not suit all communities, nor do enough parents necessarily want the kind of involvement offered by the forum approach. It is important to reflect on ends and means. A positive goal is to involve parents in aspects of planning for your service, but there are different approaches to reaching this goal.

Example from a setting

In Millom Children's Centre the team reflect on their practice through Action for Children's strong children's rights perspective. Anna Batty, the centre manager, explained how their 'Hear by Right' model – also fully adopted by Cumbria local authority – led them to explore ways to enable parent participation and to avoid any temptation to skim the surface of genuine involvement in order to tick boxes. A small group of parents came

together, with the support of a project worker, over a period of 12 weeks with the expressed goal of helping the centre to plan activities for local families. The team learned a great deal from this experience, with insights that applied to their practice as a whole.

Pound Park Children's Centre has open meetings, when there is a chance to offer ideas and opinions. Suggestions can also be posted in the suggestions box.

Parents are given a questionnaire at the end of the child's time at Pound Park. An informal group of parent volunteers organise fund raising for the centre. The possibility has been raised of creating a Family Forum, such as runs in another local Sure Start. This kind of constituted body is more formal and needs an agreed way of running. However, the current body of parents did not want this kind of involvement, so plans are on hold.

Other options in partnership working include a more formal role of parent involvement in the broader running of a setting. Some early years centres have parent representatives on management committees. Schools have to include elected parent representatives on the governing body. Good practice is to:

- Use different channels of communication to announce that nominations are welcome, since Petra's father will leave the committee this summer. Make sure that every family will have heard of the opening – not just those who look at the notice board or regularly pop in to the parents' group.

- Be ready to explain what is involved in taking up this role, and ideally put the details on paper too or on your setting's website. Potential committee members or school governors need to have a realistic understanding of the time involved and the responsibilities of the role.

Links with your practice

Any of these routes to hearing ideas and exchanging views will only work if parents can see that their comments sometimes make a difference.

- No adults are content to give their time and thoughtful opinions if nothing comes of their contribution. Nor will it promote good relations, if early years or school practitioners meet parents' queries or constructive criticism with frosty, defensive replies.

- Just as with some individual requests or clear preferences, practitioners need to be clear about what is not negotiable – in policy and practice. It would not be professional simply to announce, 'We're not allowed to do that'. Such a phrase sounds weak and also implies that the speaker might take that route, if not prevented by the invisible blockers.

- Be ready to explain on what grounds it is not possible to follow this parent's suggestion, or the exact detail of what is being proposed.

Books and websites

Athey C (1990) *Extending Thought in Young Children: A Parent-Teacher Partnership,* Paul Chapman Publishing.

Barrett H (2003) *Parenting programmes for families at risk: a source book,* National Parenting and Family Institute.

Brooker L (2002) *Starting school: young children learning cultures,* Open University Press.

Buck L, Nettleton L (2007) *Forest School in Greenwich: Principles into Practice October 2006 – July 2007.* Greenwich Council, London.

Caddell D (2001) *Working with parents: a shared understanding of the curriculum 3-5,* Learning and Teaching Scotland.

Department for Education (2012) *Statutory Framework for the Early Years Foundation Stage: Setting the Standards for Learning, Development and Care for Children from Birth to Five* (www.education.gov.uk/schools/teachingandlearning/curriculum/a0068102/early-years-foundation-stage-eyfs).

Department for Children Schools and Families (2008) *Parents as Partners in Early Learning Case Studies,* DCSF (search by title on www.dcsf.gov.uk).

Desforges C, Abouchaar A (2003) *The Impact of Parental Involvement, Parental Support and Family Education on Pupil Achievement and Adjustment: a Literature Review.* Department for Education and Skills (www.dfes.gov.uk/research/data/uploadfiles/RR433.pdf).

Effective Provision of Pre-School Education project and continuing research into primary and secondary school (access research papers via www.ioe.ac.uk/research/4585.html).

Family and Parenting Institute (www.familyandparenting.org) with links to the Early Home Learning Matters site (www.earlyhomelearning.org.uk).

Fatherhood Institute (www.fatherhoodinsitute.org) has an online library of resources and offers regular email updates.

Harris A, Goodall J *Engaging parents in raising achievement – do parents know they matter?,* DCSF, 2007 Brief No DCSF – RBW004 (www.dcsf.gov.uk/ and search by title).

Kahn T (2005) *Father's Involvement in Early Years Settings: Findings from Research,* Pre-school Learning Alliance (www.pre-school.org.uk/fathers/index.php).

Klavins L (2008) *Parents Matter: How Can Leaders Involve Parents in the Self-Evaluation Process and Further Development of Children's Centre and Extended School Services?,* National College for School Leadership (www.ncsl.org.uk/klavins-parents-matter-full.pdf).

Lindon J (2012 (revised)) *The Key Person Approach: Positive Relationships in the Early Years*, Practical Pre-School Books.

Lindon J (2012a) *What does it mean to be…?* Series of child development books, each focusing on one year in early childhood, Practical Pre-School Books.

Lindon J. (2012b) *Equality and Inclusion in Early Childhood*, Hodder Education.

Lindon J. (2012c) *Understanding Children's Behaviour 0-11 years*, Hodder Education.

Lindon J. (2012e) *Safeguarding and Child Protection 0-8 years*, Hodder Education.

Lindon J, Lindon L (2008) *Mastering Counselling Skills.* 2nd edition, Palgrave Macmillan.

National Literacy Trust – useful website with plenty to download (www.literacytrust.co.uk link to valuable www.talktoyourbaby.org.uk).

Pre-school Learning Alliance – wide range of material about partnership with fathers (www.pre-school.org.uk/fathers/).

Saunders A, Oates R, Kahn T (2009) *Hard to Reach? Engaging Fathers in Early Years Settings,* University of Derby (www.derby.ac.uk/ehs/earlyyearsresearch).

Scott W (2009) A decade of opening doors, *Early Years Educator Magazine* 11 (1).

Siren Films Ltd *Firm Foundations for Early Literacy and Supporting Early Literacy* (www.sirenfilms.co.uk).

Wheeler H, Connor J (2008) *Parents, Early Years and Learning: Activities Book for Childminders,* National Children's Bureau (www.peal.org.uk/PDF/PEALCHMD_web.pdf).

Wheeler H, Connor J (2009) *Parents, Early Years and Learning: Parents as Partners in the Early Years Foundation Stage Principles into Practice.* National Children's Bureau (More about the PEAL project on www.peal.org.uk/resources/practice-examples).

Acknowledgements

I would like to thank a considerable number of people whose ideas on partnership within early years practice have been directly helpful for this book.

I still appreciate my time spent in consultancy and training with day nurseries in the 1970s and 80s, especially from the London boroughs of Brent, Haringey and Tower Hamlets. Many of those centre leaders and early years support teams were well ahead of their time in their approach to partnership.

From more recent years I would like to thank the teams and leader/managers of the following places, given in alphabetical order: Buckingham's Nursery School (Leek, Staffordshire), Grove Nursery School (Peckham, South London – now also a Children and Family Centre), Grove House Children's Centre (Southall, West London), Petts Wood Playgroup for children with special needs (Petts Wood, Kent), Pound Park Children's Centre (Charlton, South London), RAF Marham Rainbow Centre (near Kings Lynn), Southlands Kindergarten and Crèche (Newcastle-under-Lyme), Sun Hill Infants School (New Alresford, Hampshire), Thongsley Fields Nursery and Primary School (Huntingdon, Cambridgeshire) and Windham Nursery School (Richmond, Surrey).

An additional thank you to these individuals for their time in conversation: Debbie Shepherd, 0-3s Development Officer, Thurrock about the World of Discovery sessions and contact with Sure Start Tilbury, Kim Bush, Childminding Network Co-ordinator in Charlton, south London and individual childminders: Emma Bates, Linda Crump, Hazel Jobson and Georgina Mellish-Laws.

Thanks to the practitioners involved in the Greenwich Forest School project: Liz Buck and Lucy Nettleton (who developed the project across the borough), Liz Danks (Forest School Leader at Pound Park Children's Centre), Alexa Gilbert (Forest School for under-threes), Carole Allen and Ellen Edwards (childminders actively involved in the project) and Maria O'Neill, PSLA Development Worker. Janet Hurst, Senior Parent Support Advisor at Thongsley Fields Nursery and Primary School. Anna Batty, Manager of Millom Children's Centre, Millom, Cumbria.

Any examples not attributed to specific places are drawn from my general experience. I have given names to fictional practitioners or children, because I think the brief 'for instance' then works better. None of those individuals are from any of the identified places.